# A Boomer's Guide to the 12 Steps

*V*

# A Boomer's Guide to the 12 Steps

*Stephen Roos*

HAZELDEN®

Hazelden
Center City, Minnesota 55012
hazelden.org

Library of Congress Cataloging-in-Publication Data

Roos, Stephen.
    A boomer's guide to the 12 steps / Stephen Roos.
        p.    cm.
    Includes bibliographical references.
    ISBN 978-1-59285-696-1 (softcover)
    1. Twelve-step programs.    2. Baby boom generation—Substance abuse.
    3. Baby boom generation—Alcohol use.    4. Baby boom generation—
    Conduct of life.  I. Title.
    HV4998.R66 2009
    616.86'03—dc22

                                                        2009002471

**Editor's note**
The recovering people mentioned in this book are composites. This publica-
tion is not intended as a substitute for the advice of health care professionals.
    Alcoholics Anonymous, AA, and the Big Book are registered trademarks
of Alcoholics Anonymous World Services, Inc.

13  12  11  10  09    1  2  3  4  5  6

Cover design by Mary Ann Smith
Interior design and typesetting by BookMobile Design and Publishing
Services

# Table of Contents

# Introduction

*"Anyone who says sixty is just a number has got to be kidding," says Hector R., a former schoolteacher in Fort Lauderdale. "The* AARP Bulletin *says sixty is the new thirty, but try telling that to someone who's thirty."*

ACCEPT LIFE ON LIFE'S TERMS. It's a home truth that we Boomers, the kids born between 1946 and 1964, have learned over and over again in all sorts of contexts throughout our lives. We've had to accept people for who they are—mates, kids, friends, and colleagues. We've had to accept ups and downs in our personal lives. We've had to accept ourselves too! We've faced the predicaments and calamities, some natural and others man-made, that have rocked our world—and accepted the changes and challenges they brought with them.

Now—just when we're ready to say "Enough!"—along comes one more thing we have to accept. We're turning sixty!

"I can't be sixty," says Judy D. "How can I be? I don't look sixty. I don't feel sixty."

Actually, Judy isn't sixty. She's sixty-three. Whether she's in denial about her age or just exercising the prerogative of people over fifty to lie about it, she's right that she doesn't look or feel anything like what sixty is supposed to look and feel like.

1

"When my dad was sixty, he looked old," says Hector. "He acted old too. When he retired he just sat around the house. I'm sixty now, but I'm no senior citizen."

Hector is right too. Even though the first Boomers are no longer middle-aged, we're not seniors. According to a recent poll in *USA Today*, Boomers believe old age begins at eighty. That's not just wishful Boomer thinking either. Not only do we live longer than anyone before us, we also stay healthier longer. The Boomers are, in fact, the first generation in history that can expect to live two or three decades after retirement. Unless we're struck by a devastating condition or disease, we can expect to remain vital, fit, and "pre-elderly" well into our eighties.

Being pioneers, of course, is nothing new for Boomers. We have been trendsetters since we were born. After all, we grew up in a world that was vastly different from our parents'. The 1950s, '60s, and '70s were an era of unprecedented economic growth and extraordinary social change. The civil rights movement, the women's movement, and gay liberation shaped our attitudes and lifestyles as dramatically as the post–World War II economic boom did.

We've had more options, greater opportunities, and considerably higher expectations than any generation ever. But as the first of us apply for Social Security benefits, many of us are bewildered by what looms ahead. How can we *not* be preoccupied by worries about our money, our health, our relationships, and our work, as we enter a new, uncharted stage of life? Accustomed as we are to thinking positively, looking good, and taking a generally proactive role in life, for many of us, it's as hard to share about the downside going on inside us as it is to ask others what's really going on inside them.

"I don't want to seem like I'm complaining," says Jowin H., "especially when so many people have it worse than I do."

Says Mack O., "My wife and my kids and buddies from work are used to me complaining about this and that, but I'd be embarrassed to talk to them about how scared I am about the future."

"My friends think I'm on top of things," says Charlene P. "If I told my friends how I really feel, they just wouldn't know how to handle it."

Though Charlene, Mack, Jowin, and Hector are in Twelve Steps programs, Judy isn't. But even in Twelve Step programs, where you are *supposed* to talk about anything and everything, you can feel reluctant to speak about the challenges and feelings that come with turning sixty.

Olga Z. has been in Alcoholics Anonymous for eighteen years. "That's three or four meetings a week most of the time. It adds up to something like three thousand meetings. I thought I had said everything I was going to say—twice."

"I was there for the newcomer," says Robert G. "I tried to keep it upbeat. Besides, who wanted to hear about my crap? What good was it going to do anyone, anyway?"

Says Sally B., "Most of the gals in my OA [Overeaters Anonymous] group are my daughter's age. You think I'm going to ask them for advice? Besides, at this point in my life, I was much more comfortable giving it. Someone convinced me to attend a Step workshop. That's where I started to make a more conscious effort to connect with other men and women my age. They were working the Steps in the context of who they are now, talking about the things I wasn't talking about. It helped reinvigorate my whole program."

Robert was also at the Step workshop: he had relapsed after many years of sobriety. "I'd gone through the Steps before the first couple years I was in program," he says. "I still used some of them, but basically I was on automatic pilot. But when I came back from my slip, I knew I had to get into the Steps again. Powerless had a whole new meaning to me at sixty than it did when I was thirty-five and first came into the program," he adds, chuckling a bit, "and that was just the beginning."

Not all Boomers in the program are old-timers. Craig W. is in his mid-fifties. He has been battling his addictions, alcohol and more recently crystal meth, for more than thirty years, but has been in the Crystal Meth Anonymous (CMA) program just a year. Hector didn't develop a drinking problem until he retired. Although the statistics aren't in yet, he seems to be among the growing number of social drinkers and even non-drinkers who start to drink alcoholically in their fifties and sixties. As Hector says, "The Steps helped me look at who I was—without beating up on myself. I'd been afraid to look, I guess."

Today, a wide variety of programs take a Twelve Step approach to recovery. Many of them address various types of substance use—the original Twelve Step program is Alcoholics Anonymous (AA), but others include Narcotics Anonymous (NA) and groups for users of specific drugs, e.g., Cocaine Anonymous (CA). The Overeaters Anonymous program is known as OA. Some Twelve Step programs address other addictive behaviors—gambling or compulsive sex, for example. Most of these programs share some common elements, such as frequent peer-led group meetings and a sponsorship tradition, whereby newcomers are mentored by more experienced members. And for decades, the Al-Anon and Nar-Anon programs have offered recovery support for family members and others who are affected by a person's addiction. In this book, we'll discuss the Steps as they appear in the recovery text *Alcoholics Anonymous*, known as the Big Book. Two of the Steps refer to alcohol specifically—but in fact all of them apply to any addictive substance or behavior.

You don't need to be in a Twelve Step program to use the

Steps in your life. Says Judy, "I was never in a Twelve Step program, but one of my girlfriends told me she thought I was getting addicted to cosmetic surgery the way she had been to prescription drugs. She was going to the Step workshop after we'd been out to dinner one night, and I tagged along. I didn't realize she had set me up, but I'm glad she did now."

Jowin agrees. "My kids, they're in their thirties, and one of them has a gambling problem," he says. "I used to go to open Gamblers Anonymous meetings and Al-Anon to show my support for my son. I don't suffer from addiction myself, but the Steps helped me recognize the problems I have. They also help me with ways to deal with the problems. I mean, what's the point of recognizing a problem if you can't solve it?"

And so it goes. The Steps are immensely practical tools that help us to live sane, productive lives, whether we are old-timers or newcomers to the programs, or even if we have never been to a Twelve Step meeting and have no plans to attend one. As we grow, we change. We're not the people we were ten years ago, even five years ago. And we're not changing into the people our parents were when they were our age.

The Steps can prove to be just the guide we need as we pioneer in territory that no generation has ever explored before. As Robert says, "Thanks to the Steps, these really are turning out to be the best years of my life."

### Meet the Experts: The Recovering Men and Women Who Shared Their Stories

**Charlene P.** In Al-Anon for eight years, Charlene has identified strongly as a housewife and mom. When her husband died just after their fortieth wedding anniversary, he left hardly enough money for her to live on. She has few marketable skills and is as anxious about finding a job as she is adamant about not accepting help from her now grown-up children.

**Craig W.** Sober a year, Craig is recovering from a crystal meth addiction and only just beginning to deal with child abuse issues. Now in his mid-fifties and HIV positive, he's a model and cater waiter who's only just beginning to face the fact that his compulsive partying has derailed him from the acting career he'd always dreamed of.

**Hector R.** Sober in AA just 18 months, Hector developed a drinking problem when he retired. A former high school Spanish teacher, he's a loner who faces a life of total isolation. He's dealing with prostate cancer now—and he's scared.

**Jowin H.** A salesman, Jowin is married with two kids, a son who has trouble with a gambling addiction and a daughter he has spoiled rotten. He got into Al-Anon when his son got into Gamblers Anonymous (GA). Jowin uses the Steps to deal with issues at home (his adultery included) and at work.

**Judy D.** A mother and a grandmother, Judy is recently divorced and bitter. She devoted herself to being the perfect corporate mate, credits herself with much of her ex-husband's success, and can't help nursing a grievance about her ex-husband's former secretary—his new, younger trophy wife. Although she drank and smoked pot in the 1960s, she did not become addicted to either. After her divorce she became addicted to plastic surgery, which is when a friend introduced her to the Twelve Steps. Although she is still not in one of the programs, she does follow the Steps.

**Mack O.** A used-car salesman, Mack has been in the AA program for six years and has college-age kids. Without telling his wife, he took over management of his and his wife's retirement funds and lost most of the family's life savings. Coming clean with her was one of the hardest things Mack ever had to do. Now approaching retirement age, Mack doubts he'll be able to afford to retire.

**Olga Z.** Olga has been sober in AA for eighteen years. A Russian immigrant, she was born poor but became tough and enormously successful in real estate. Always proud of her fierce independence, she never allowed a romantic relationship to come before her drive to achieve the American dream.

**Robert G.** He had been sober in AA for thirty years when he slipped. Back in recovery after six months, Robert is now in therapy and on meds. A banker, he took early retirement, never anticipating that it would precipitate a personal crisis.

**Sally B.** At the age of fifty-eight, Sally has been involved in Overeaters Anonymous for fifteen years. She is married, has two grown-up kids, and is the main caregiver for her elderly father who is suffering from Alzheimer's. She has an at-home business making gourmet fudge. Almost predictably, she has become diabetic and worries that she will not be there to care for her father. It's only when she does her Fourth Step that she realizes how deeply resentful she is as well.

# STEP ONE

*"We admitted we were powerless over alcohol—
that our lives had become unmanageable."*

WHAT ARE YOU POWERLESS OVER? A drug? A behavior? Your temper? The economy? Gravity? When you find you are powerless over something—or someone—do you readily admit it? Is that getting easier as you get older? Or has time made it harder for you to admit when you're beat? Has your powerlessness ever made your life—or some aspect of your life—unmanageable? Is it unmanageable now?

Don't be too quick to say no. Denial comes in many shapes and sizes, and we all experience it at one time or another. Sometimes, a bit of denial can get us through a tough situation. Left unchecked, however, denial can turn a tough situation into a disaster. Age brings wisdom, no doubt, but it's no guarantee that we'll be able to see through our denial. By the time we reach our fifties and sixties, we may be so adept at certain forms of denial that it becomes an involuntary response. In fact, we may even claim that age exempts us from certain problems.

"I thought alcoholism was like acne," says Hector. "You had to be a kid to get it. I didn't drink or do drugs when I was young. In fact, I didn't have my first drink till I was forty. I didn't have my first hangover till six years ago. Even when things got really bad, I thought I was too old to become an alcoholic."

How many of us have learned that you can't be too old to develop problems with sex or money? How many of us are still going to Al-Anon to learn how to deal with our powerlessness over other people? For some of us, the substance we are powerless over is food. "When my friends told me they were worried about my eating, I just pretended I didn't hear them," says Sally. "If they said it again, I stopped seeing them too. I wasn't addicted to food. I just liked food better than other people did."

Can someone even be addicted to plastic surgery? "I was deeply hurt when my husband decided he wanted out of the marriage," says Judy. "Who wouldn't be? When I discovered plastic surgery, I felt I had found the solution to all my problems. I decided to have my eyes done, but my doctor convinced me to have a full face-lift. Then I wanted to have some body work. My insurance wouldn't cover it, so I had to pay for it myself. I'd gone through a major part of my divorce settlement when I realized I was out of control."

"Who would have thought the Internet could become an addiction?" asks Mack. "It sounds absurd, but I was spending so much time online trading stock from my 401-K that my life was becoming unmanageable. That led to some serious problems in my finances and in my marriage."

### The Power of Denial

But whatever the substance or behavior, we can always find a way to deny it's a problem. Olga thought her superior willpower would keep her out of harm's way. "I could quit any time I wanted. That was what proved I wasn't an alcoholic. My doctor told me I had to stop drinking," she explains. "That was it. No more drinking. I got through two days without booze and, believe me, those were the two longest days of my life. The third day I drank. Even though my health was in serious jeopardy, it was a conscious choice. Booze was more important to me than my health. That's my denial system killing me."

Robert thought he was too smart, too rich, and sober too long to drink again. He had just celebrated the thirtieth anniversary of his sobriety when he slipped. "I knew the Big Book by heart. I could say the Serenity Prayer [see page 113] in my sleep. I thought I was just too damn smart to go back to drinking. I still had money in the bank. That was my rationale. I found out that some of the richest, most successful people in the world are active alcoholics. Also, some of the smartest and most talented people. The hardest-working."

"I was badly in debt," says Craig. "I knew I wasn't the sharpest tack in the toolbox, but I wasn't living on the streets. I attended my first Twelve Step meeting when I was twenty-five, but I've never put together more than six months of continuous sobriety before. But as long as I could point the finger at someone who was worse off than I was, I figured I was okay."

Unmanageability, however, is as hard to admit as powerlessness, especially at our age. Now that we're older, we're supposed to know better. The truth is that very often our lives can look manageable, even when inside we're spinning out of control.

"My friends spend a lot of their time talking about how stupid young people are today," says Charlene. "How they get into trouble and can't get themselves out. How was I going to explain to my friends that I was screwed up too?"

"I never drugged—only drank," Mack says. "I didn't gamble. How could it be bad if it looked so good? I wanted to die, but even at my worst my life looked manageable. But I was totally out of control with money. I had lied to my wife about it too."

Often we're just kidding ourselves. "Well, I have to admit my life *looked* unmanageable," says Judy, smiling ruefully. "But *I* looked fabulous. That's what I told myself, anyway. As long as I looked good, it didn't matter how messed up life was."

Sometimes feelings can overwhelm us and make our lives unmanageable—even if we have a lifetime of dealing with them. You don't have to have an addiction to have problems with depression, anxiety, resentment, fear, and low self-esteem. They can get the better of all of us from time to time.

"I was the most capable person in my admittedly not too capable family," says Sally. "Who else was supposed to take care of my father when he developed Alzheimer's? I just couldn't imagine putting him in a home. When some of the gals asked me how I did it, I told them that you could do anything if you put your mind to it. I acted like it was no problem at all. I was in total denial about how angry and resentful I was feeling."

Fortunately, Sally came out of her denial before her resentment got the best of her. Robert wasn't so lucky. "I kept telling myself I had luxury problems," he says. "I had worked hard all my life and it was my turn to sit back and enjoy. But I had a bad case of depression. My doctor recommended antidepressants and therapy, but I told him I wasn't that bad. Then the depression got worse, and that led me back to drinking."

We can feel overwhelmed by health issues. We don't have to be out of control with spending to know how money problems can make our lives unmanageable. Some of us find ourselves alone for the first time in our lives and overwhelmed with feelings of loneliness. Step One can prove invaluable in helping us admit our powerlessness over these feelings and how unmanageable those feelings have made our lives.

"We went through most of our savings when my husband was sick," says Charlene. "When he died, there was nothing left. I told myself some money would turn up eventually. I'd never gotten a degree, and I didn't have any experience working outside my home. I bought lottery tickets every week, thinking that was how God was going to take care of me. It wasn't till I was totally broke that I got real. Thanks to my denial, things got a lot worse before they got better. It was a tough situation, but it didn't have to be that tough!"

"There's a history of prostate cancer in my family," says Hector. "When my doctor told me my PSA was up, I just put it out of my mind. Didn't make an appointment with a urologist. Didn't even think about it. A man my age in AA told me I better check it out. It turned out I was sick, but fortunately, they got it early. I realized that I needed to practice Step One in every area of my life, not just my drinking and drugging."

"It took me a long time to admit I had problems that were making my life unmanageable," says Sally. "But the day I did, my life started to change for the better."

By denying our powerlessness as well as the unmanageability of our lives, we are also denying ourselves the possibility of solving our problems and moving on. For Twelve-Steppers, sobriety is not just about putting down the drink or drug and learning how to stay out of trouble with money, sex, and relationships. It's about dealing with the anxieties and fears that have plagued us all along and discovering a happier, more joyous, and freer life than we ever imagined.

It's never too early to start, and it's never too late. Taking Step One can be the watershed, the decisive turning point for anyone at any age. Before we can reclaim our true power, we have to face our powerlessness over the addictive substances or behaviors that are controlling our lives. There's no age limit on that life lesson.

"I guess I thought that once I hit sixty, life would just naturally be a downward spiral," says Mack. "It's a two-way spiral, but before I can start going up again, I have to admit how unmanageable it's been for me."

## STEP TWO

*"Came to believe that a Power greater
than ourselves could restore us to sanity."*

"THIS STEP USED TO BUG ME," says Hector. "I thought it was just plain wrong to assume that I automatically had a problem with sanity. I came to AA because I wanted to stop drinking, not because I was crazy."

Most of us come into recovery, as Hector did, with the belief that we are about as sane as the next guy and most of the people we know. Even those of us who had a problem with drinking and drugging would be hard-pressed to see ourselves as "insane," even when we drank and used.

Our family, friends, and coworkers would be inclined to agree. It's one thing to admit we're powerless, but what's the point of the "sanity clause"? Understandably, some of us may resist, even challenge, Step Two at the beginning. But considering the harm we've done to ourselves and others, if our history of denying our powerlessness and our lives' unmanageability doesn't constitute some form of insanity, what does? Would anyone actually choose to "let" one's life become so unmanageable?

Did we ever intend to get into trouble? Even when we'd been through the worst of it, even when a wealth of life experience proved conclusively that our way of thinking and handling life invariably led to trouble, how many of us still fervently maintained that we were doing okay, that we didn't have a problem? Even after we have taken Step One and admitted the unmanageability, isn't it remarkable how our denial can reactivate in a flash? Isn't it amazing how easily we can "forget" how powerless we are and how unmanageable our lives used to be—and still are? That's the insanity.

"What helped me was looking up *sanity* in the dictionary," says Hector. "It means health. Today I look at things as either mentally healthy or mentally unhealthy. That makes Step Two very accessible for me."

## Your Inner Addict Is the Voice of Insanity

Diseases can do any number of things, but addictive diseases may well be the only ones that seem to talk. If you have heard your disease telling you one more drink wouldn't hurt or recommending the marijuana maintenance plan, you know firsthand that the "disease" is actually the voice of insanity within you.

"After a couple of weeks in the program, I was feeling a helluva lot better," says Craig. "But I wanted to use. No particular reason. It wasn't a bad day at all. I just wanted to do a couple of lines. That's crazy. After what I went through when I drank and drugged, that's got to be the disease talking."

If you haven't heard your disease speak, you may find it manifesting more subtly in unhealthy attitudes, reactions, and even beliefs. What about depression and mood swings that can set us up for a slip?

"I could see how this Step could apply when I first came to OA," says Sally. "I was bouncing off the walls. But frankly, I didn't see how it applied to me once I'd been in the program a while. I overreacted to so many things. I thought it was just because I was more sensitive than other people. Fortunately, my sponsor helped me look at it as unhealthy thinking."

Says Robert, "I know everyone goes through bad patches, but when my bad patch after I retired turned into a way of life, I should have recognized it as a serious emotional problem. Was I nuts? No, but I wasn't healthy emotionally. I learned the hard way that this is one Step you need to keep working as long as you're sober."

As we follow the Twelve Steps, we almost invariably begin to improve. The intense emotional swings, and the noisy, sometimes violent outbursts that often accompanied them, dissipate or even disappear. Our progress is definitely worth noting, but we still have our issues. Even when we seem to be behaving like perfectly sane men and women, our insanity can manifest quietly in our feelings, our beliefs, and our attitudes.

"To me, low self-esteem is insane," says Sally. "It's the voice that I'm not enough, that I don't deserve what I have, that I'm going to lose it all."

"I see the insanity in the way I'm still always comparing myself to others," says Jowin. "I'm always a whole lot better than everybody else, or a whole lot worse. Either way, I know where that voice is coming from."

"It's amazing how little it takes to trigger my feelings," says Charlene. "Someone doesn't smile back to me on the street, and I feel hurt or sometimes I feel angry. It's all about me all the time. That's not healthy thinking."

"I had to face the fact I had become the proverbial human 'doing,' not a human being," Sally points out. "Definitely, I needed to be restored to sanity."

"I realized I was a compulsive fretter," says Jowin. "My fretting got worse as I got older too. When I was young, I used to worry about paying the rent. Now I worry about paying off the loan for my swimming pool. I'm the constant. It's about me, not the rent or the swimming pool."

It is not insane to worry. It's normal. It's even healthy insofar as worry can propel us toward some action that can solve the problem at hand. But excessive worry can trigger a depressive, obsessive streak in us.

"My blood pressure goes up thirty points when my doctor checks it," says Charlene. "It's called 'white jacket anxiety.' When I was young, I expected to be healthy. But Step Two is teaching me the difference between the worry that gets me to the doctor, which I think is sane, and the fretting I do after the doctor has given me a clean bill of health, which is insanity."

"It's insane that I thought I had to do it alone," Olga says. "It's even more insane that I wanted to. I know because I tried. But there are a lot of things I can't do all by myself."

Hoping to be restored to sanity is one thing, but believing it is quite another. For many of us, coming to believe that a Power greater than ourselves can restore us to sanity reflects a major change in our belief system.

Says Charlene, "I just had to be open-minded. Before I started the Steps, if I had a problem, I lived with it. That's nuts, but that's how it was for me. Step Two showed me that I had to be open to solving problems. I had to be open to receiving help from others, whether it was my friends, my family, or even a God whom I didn't happen to believe in."

Our feelings are a manifestation of our beliefs. Do some of your insane feelings come from some insane beliefs?

### We Get to Define Our Higher Power

"The whole 'Power greater than ourselves' business was hard to swallow," Mack says. "I'm a very self-reliant guy. We lived in a gorgeous house. We had three cars. We vacationed all over the world. I never needed a Power greater than myself for my sanity or for anything else. But then I screwed up with my retirement account and only a Power greater than myself could save me."

"I watch the miracle healers on TV," says Sally. "I see a man of the cloth put his hand on someone's forehead and suddenly the person can walk or see or hear again. In the movies, there's thunder and the heavens part and the sun shines through. Frankly, I was waiting for something like that to happen."

For Sally it was a major relief to find that a Power greater than ourselves does not necessarily require a Hollywood film studio's special effects department. Our Higher Power can work so subtly that sometimes we do not see it happening. In fact, sometimes we don't recognize it until after it has happened.

"What happened on my last day drinking?" Olga asks. "Was it any different from the day before that? Were you different? Did it just happen out of the blue? It wasn't the first day I wished I could do something about my drinking. Why couldn't I put the drink down all the other days I had wished I could stop? Why did it happen that day and not the day before? I'll never know for sure, but for me it was an opportunity to consider the possibility of a Power greater than myself. No matter what I believed, I had to consider the possibility that there is some power operating in my life, and that power is a benevolent one."

Step Two shows not only how to recognize our mental state, but also how to work toward a solution. Judy goes to therapy. Robert's doctor prescribed antidepressants, which he takes as prescribed. Clearly, Step Two doesn't replace our need for medical professionals any more than it replaces our need for financial experts when we have money problems, or our need for a professional plumber when a faucet leak is performing Chinese water torture on us.

As invaluable as therapy and state-of-the-art medicines can be, neither Robert nor Judy mistakes them for a Higher Power. But they do recognize these solutions can be the result of that power's guidance. For some people, this Power greater than themselves is called God. Some people feel the Power greater than themselves is a Higher Power who speaks through other people. This includes those who don't believe in a personal God and find a Power greater than themselves in their AA group. Our spirituality is a deeply personal matter, and it can develop in any number of different and equally effective ways.

But there's no denying the changes that we see every day, in ourselves and the people around us, when we commit—or recommit—to working this Step. "Before I got into the Steps, every feeling I had was a fact," says Mack. "If I felt like I was better than everyone, I acted like I was better. If I felt bad, I was bad. It was crazy. I see that now. Every feeling I have isn't a fact. This Step has helped teach me the difference. It's changed the way I think. That's affected my beliefs and also my behavior."

When Jowin's son got into trouble with his gambling debts, he moved back home. Jowin felt obligated to take care of his thirty-seven-year-old son, mostly out of guilt: he thought that it was probably his own fault that his son was addicted to gambling. "It seemed to me that I was being a good parent," says Jowin. "I had equated being guilt-ridden with being good. That's insane. The Second Step helped me to see that."

Behavior can change, even when we are in our fifties or sixties. So can feelings. So can beliefs that generate those feelings. That's what recovery is all about. Step Two—being open to the possibility that a Power greater than you exists and can be a source of strength and hope—is key to initiating these changes.

*"Made a decision to turn our will and our lives over to the care of God* as we understood Him."

BY THE TIME WE'RE IN OUR FIFTIES AND SIXTIES, many of us are generally sick of debating the whole God issue. We have had a lot of time to mull it over, and whatever we believe—or don't believe—we're pretty secure, perhaps unyielding, in the conclusions we have reached. But no matter where we're at or where we're coming from, working the Third Step means reexamining our belief systems and being open to change.

Before we decide where we're going here—or decide we're not going anywhere—we need to spend a little time considering where we're coming from. There are plenty of people on the planet who profess their belief in God. But the actions some of them take in the name of their God are incredibly cruel, vengeful, and intolerant. Is that the God whose care we want to turn our will and our lives over to? Then there are the people who adamantly deny the existence of God. Sometimes they can sound as zealous as the believers.

Most of us fall somewhere between those two extremes. If we do believe in a Higher Power, how much do we believe? How often do we act on that belief? Do we act like people who believe we have a benevolent Higher Power looking out after us? Do we treat other people as the beloved children of a Higher Power, as we believe (or hope) ourselves to be? Do we trust? Do we care? Do we dare to love?

## We All Have Higher Powers

Whether we care to admit it or not, we all have Higher Powers. Make a list. Add anything that has controlled your life. How about ambition? What about lust or vanity? What about fear? If someone out there didn't worship money, who would have ever called a dollar the "almighty buck"? Did you ever turn your will and your life over to another person? Maybe a boss?

Or maybe somebody you fell in love with became your Higher Power. Hasn't fear ruled our lives at one time or another? Fear wasn't necessarily our God, but it certainly was a Power greater than ourselves, and our belief in that power affected (if not controlled) our feelings and our behavior.

If alcohol and other drugs got you into trouble, leading you places you never intended to go and prompting you to do things you never would have done if you'd been clean and sober, you probably have those substances on your list too.

"Well, it's not as though I prayed to a bottle of vodka," Olga laughs. "But I have to admit that on more than one occasion I did speak to one. Vodka became my best friend over the years. When I was younger, I had girlfriends I'd talk to when I was depressed or feeling down, but as time went on, it was easier to drink. Alcohol just made my fear go away. It was the one thing I could count on to pick me up when I was down. I was grateful to vodka. Before I realized it was killing me, I thought it was what got me through. That's a Higher Power, I suppose."

"The first time I saw this Step, I just knew it meant trouble," says Craig. "I'd never thought about God since I went to Sunday school. Religion just wasn't part of my adult life, I guess, and it never occurred to me that maybe I had reached an age where it could become meaningful to me again."

Small wonder. Craig had been abused when he was a child by one of the priests in his family church. When he was still in his teens, he knew he was gay. When he tried to talk about it, the same priest told him that sex between men was a sin. Craig's story may be a worst-case scenario, but it's amazing how many men and women have negative feelings about religions of all kinds. Any number of Twelve-Steppers identify themselves only half-jokingly as "recovering Catholics" or "recovering fundamentalists," for example. Some even blame God and their churches for their drinking and drugging problems. Even among those whose experience with God and with formal religions is less dire, it's not unusual for newly sober people to approach this Step with serious trepidation. Turning your life over to the care of anything or anyone is a staggering concept, no matter where you're coming from. "For me, the key was the word 'care,'" says Olga. "That made all the difference. It says God is going to care for me, not judge me or punish me."

"When I was younger, I did go to church," says Sally. "I did pray that God would make me feel comfortable, but it didn't happen. It was food that did the job for me. I guess you could say it was like a Higher Power to me. At the beginning, I mean. It didn't stay that way for long. But once that happened, I was hooked."

Living up to expectations. That's nothing new. What parent wouldn't want his or her child to succeed in life—to be an all-star athlete and a great student, get a great job, have a great marriage, and produce super kids? For Boomers, there's a twist. What might have seemed like pipe dreams for previous generations were for us realizable goals—if only we worked hard enough, studied long enough, behaved. If we failed to live up to our goals, or to the ones our parents set for us, we had only ourselves to blame.

It couldn't have been a sharper contrast to where our own parents were coming from. So many of them had come of age during the Great Depression, when living indoors and keeping yourself fed counted as a major achievement. During the boom times that followed World War II, parents themselves were achieving so much more than their own parents had. They assumed their kids would do at least as well as they had, if not better.

All too often, the expectations we Boomers grew up with have led us to place unrealistic demands on ourselves and take a diminished view of what a Higher Power could do in our personal lives. When Sally's life turned out to be more real than sitcoms like *Leave It to Beaver* or *Father Knows Best,* she felt she had failed. She felt her Higher Power had failed her. Even when reality lives up to our expectations, the result can play havoc with our spiritual lives. Robert had the job, the wife, and the kids. When he was in his mid-thirties, he had the beautiful second home by a lake and three cars too. "I don't know what exactly I was supposed to feel. It's patronizing, I know, but I envied the people out there who still thought making a success of themselves in life would make them feel complete. They had something to look forward to. I didn't. I tried religion, but how could God compete with alcohol?" he asks. "Two shots of whiskey and I was okay. God never worked as fast as that."

Mack grew up in a fundamentalist religion. "All I heard about was how much God hated sinners. I didn't know exactly what my sins were, but I was sure God did. I was scared of God. When my older brother got killed in Vietnam in the 1970s, I felt God had abandoned me and my family."

"Indifference," says Judy. "My grandparents were believers. My parents were respectful, but it seemed with every generation our family just got less and less interested. Frankly, I just don't think my family felt we needed a Higher Power in our lives. It seemed we were doing just fine without one. I told myself I was doing fine, too. And I was, until everything fell apart and I felt I was too old to put it back together. Age usurped my powers."

"I was pretty much from the *If there's a God, how could he let so many people suffer?* school," Sally says. "I just didn't think about God, but I did develop a certain disdain, maybe even contempt, for people who believed in God. They struck me as not-so-bright, totally unquestioning dullards. It took me almost a lifetime to realize that's not necessarily true."

Many of us find we have inadvertently become our own Higher Power. This can be especially true for those of us who grew up in dysfunctional homes. "I grew up going to church three times a week," says Jowin. "My church was very involved in the civil rights movement. That was very important to me, of course. But when my dad left, my mom said it was because there were just too many mouths to feed. I guess that meant it was my fault. When we lost our house, it was up to me to find a new one. I was only fifteen too. Believe it or not, I did get us a new home. That was how I learned I had to be the Higher Power. No one else was stepping up to the plate. But after all, how many years can a man be his own Higher Power? I was the Higher Power for my family, but it's kind of lonely to play God."

"I guess when you come right down to it, I was mad at God," says Craig. "I'm HIV positive. Half my friends died of AIDS in the 1980s. I didn't think it was fair. I still don't think it's fair."

Contempt. Fear. Indifference. Anger. There seem to be any number of reasons we are disinclined, even hostile, toward almost anything having to do with God. Wouldn't it be easier just to forego this Step? Why not just move along to the next one? Besides, there are some, if not many, atheists and agnostics in Twelve Step programs. The AA Big Book even has a chapter for agnostics. Clearly, belief in a Higher Power is not compulsory in Twelve Step programs. But exploring where we are coming from in terms of spirituality, and learning, as many of us do, that spirituality does not have to be linked to any religion can be enormously helpful explorations in themselves.

## Asking for Help—and Then Accepting It

Consider the "care" issue. Women and men who come to the Twelve Step programs characteristically have distorted attitudes about care—giving it and receiving it. Some of us give too much. Others seem to be unhealthily dependent on other people for care. By just about anyone's standards, we don't seem to take very good care of ourselves. Some of us never learned. Some of us learned but forgot. Now, as we gain the perspective of gathering years, we are recognizing that we need to change, and that may mean being willing to accept help from sources we never considered before: from people we looked down on previously, from institutions we disdained, and even from a Higher Power many of us believed never existed. If we entertain the possibility of help from a Higher Power, mysterious and elusive as that can be, we are in effect decreasing our dependence from the plethora of lower powers—people, fears, drugs, and so on—that we had previously turned our will and our lives over to.

"What got me thinking was hearing the other people talking about the Higher Powers in their life," says Sally. "I'd never imagined a God who was so benevolent, so personally involved with people. I saw how just thinking someone was looking out for you could change the way you felt and the way you acted. I tried it, little by little. At first, it seemed like I was copping out, becoming a little girl again and expecting somebody to take care of me. And I knew I was much too old for that! But I came to realize that the older I get, the more I'm going to have to accept being taken care of."

"I sat around waiting for a bolt of lightning to strike," says Hector. "I waited and waited for some sign. It was on my ninetieth day that I realized that the sign had been there for ninety days. I just hadn't noticed it. The Higher Power of my understanding is all about process, and it's a process I may not see."

"For some people, faith is a 24/7 thing," says Robert. "They believe absolutely and all the time too. Frankly, I was always a little scornful of the total certainty I see in the people on religious TV. I was also a little intimidated. If I couldn't believe as absolutely as they do, then my faith couldn't be the real thing. I'm as compulsive about comparing myself to other people as I was about my drinking. I had to learn I couldn't compare my faith with anyone else's. I do learn from other people's faith, however."

"My faith is a growing thing," says Sally. "Every day is a new day. You know, the issues I deal with today are very often the same issues I have dealt with all my life. But I've never been fifty-eight before and dealt with money problems. I've never been fifty-eight and dealt with my kids or with my dad before. I've never been fifty-eight and dealt with these particular health problems before. My Higher Power has been there for me all along, so I'm reasonably confident that She'll be here for me today, but I'm an alcoholic and so there's always that lingering fear that my Higher Power won't show up for me tomorrow."

"It's odd, but I had come to believe in spiritual practices first," says Judy. "I learned about meditating first. I had learned something about meditation back in the 1960s when the Maharishi [transcendental meditation teacher Maharishi Mahesh Yogi] came to our campus. I was smoking a lot of pot back then, and then I got serious about my drinking. I stopped meditating, of course, but when I got sober, I went back to it. That was important. It was the only thing outside of the meetings that could quiet my mind. Then of course, I just naturally started talking to the cosmos. I realized that could be considered prayer. I found it was a very peaceful, restorative space for me. That's God for me."

"I have a disease that wakes up fifteen minutes before I do," says Mack. "It's my self-centered fear calling out to me, and a Higher Power is the best tool I have to deal with that. Believe me; nothing works like my knees hitting the floor as soon as I wake up. Otherwise, I get swamped in my own negativity even before I have brushed my teeth. When I was young and a real go-getter, I was so busy with my job, my family, and stuff that I didn't have time to think. Now I do, and my thoughts are naturally negative. That's why I need help from a Higher Power. I heard someone say G.O.D. stood for 'good orderly direction,' and that was something I could handle."

"It's the people in my OA group," says Sally, "so I guess they are my Higher Power. A least my Higher Power seems to speak to me through them."

"It's never a done deal," says Robert. "It's always a deal in the doing. What's key is that I acknowledge my need for help. For someone who would rather drink himself into an early grave than ask for help, that has got to be a big deal."

"For someone who would ask any lower power I went home with to take care of me," says Charlene, "asking a Higher Power is a big, healthy step forward. If your church works for you, that's super. But for me, church got in the way of my spirituality. Learning that you don't need to be religious to be spiritual was a real breakthrough for me. It changed everything."

For people who have been their own Higher Powers, it's a relief. "From personal experience, I can tell you being God is a lot of hard work," says Jowin, smiling. "It was a blow to find out I wasn't God. But after the shock wore off, I found it made life a lot easier."

It's also about now. For all your regrets and resentments about the past, for all your fears about the future, it's possible to begin to believe that you are being taken care of this very moment. And no matter what you may be currently struggling with—medical treatments, a financial crunch, a relationship that has stretched you to the limit—you can start to trust that in this very moment you are safe. You will *know* it too. It could be because, consciously or unconsciously, you made a decision to turn your will and your life over to a Higher Power of your understanding.

# STEP FOUR

*"Made a searching and
fearless moral inventory of ourselves."*

NO GENERATION HAS EVER BEEN SO GUNG HO on self-awareness as we Boomers have been. By now, you may well feel you've done enough self-examination to last a lifetime or two. But even if you've been in therapy, even if you've done this Step previously in a Twelve Step program, it makes sense to give yourself a thorough Fourth Step checkup now, as you embark on a whole new stage of your life.

As we transition from one stage to another, we may feel like strangers in a strange new land. We may begin to think we're strangers even to ourselves. Step Four is a chance to reaffirm our identities as we experience the life changes that come with getting older. It's about preparing for change.

Do you feel you're unprepared for the next leg of the journey? Do you think you're too set in your ways and already too old to change? Doing Step Four at this time in your life can help you see how far you've come since you were twenty, thirty, or even fifty. You can see how you dealt with life changes in the past and, more often than not, you may be pleasantly surprised by how often you have risen to the occasion.

Remember to keep the focus on yourself when doing this Step. When someone asks how you're doing, do you find yourself naturally talking about your kids, your grandkids, your neighbor, everyone *but* yourself? Do you find yourself becoming preoccupied with what everyone else thinks of you? Step Four can be a way to train yourself to honestly see yourself—again, or maybe for the first time—for who you really are.

But Step Four is not therapy. If you want to explore how you got where you are today, that's important to do. If you want to spend time figuring out how the significant people in your life have affected you, that can be important too. But Step Four can be as simple as making a comprehensive itemized list of the qualities—both negative and positive—that define who you are now.

It's not about beating up on yourself, and it's not an ego trip either. This Step won't be very helpful if you use this time to rationalize or justify the things you're not so proud of. This Step is an opportunity to look at yourself in a critical but nonjudgmental way.

It's not your ex-partner's inventory or the inventory of the lady from the IRS who audited last year's tax returns. Even if you were allowed in their heads or hearts, this time stick to your own.

### Taking Inventory

The Big Book offers what is probably still the best formula for doing a "searching and fearless" inventory. Our problems and character defects generally are demonstrated in our relationships where we have felt resentment, the "'number one' offender." That's why chapter 5, "How It Works," recommends that we make a list of the people in our lives with whom we've experienced some resentment (and for the purposes of this "tuneup," this includes ourselves), and ask ourselves, "Where had we been selfish, dishonest, self-seeking and frightened?"

Who are the important people in your life you'll want to include on your list? You might start with

- spouse, partner, or significant other
- children and grandchildren
- friends
- colleagues at work, if you're still employed
- family of origin, especially your parents or other aging relatives

Now explore the most challenging issues you may be facing in these relationships as you age—including your relationship with yourself. Consider issues such as

- sex, especially with your spouse or partner, but also any past issues with others
- money and financial security
- your health, especially your fear of diminishing capacity, both mental and physical
- your changing role as a contributor to your family, community, or society as you age
- your use of free time—for example, social life, hobbies, and other pleasurable activities

Remember to list both your defects—areas where you need to improve—*and* your strengths, those successes and personality traits that make you feel good about yourself and give you the tools to weather the challenges you're facing at this time in your life.

### Tips from Some Experts

"I remember my first Fourth Step," Olga says. "It was almost a hundred pages long. Handwritten. It was everything that ever happened to me, year by year. It wasn't until I got to the Fifth Step and started reading it aloud that I realized a simple list would have been a lot easier and also a lot more useful."

"As I recall, I devoted a lot of my first Fourth Step to how various people, my wife and kids included, had forced me to do the crap I did," says Mack. "Even when I was the perpetrator, I was still a victim. That taught me something I didn't much want to know about myself."

Sally joined a Step study group last year. "When I first did this Step, it was eleven years ago and I was in my forties. I wrote a lot about my mom and dad and my husband and my kids, but hardly anything about me. I know why too. I was afraid to identify myself. This time, I wrote about me. I found out that I'm a hard-working, caring person. Yes, I have some problem areas that I need to work on before I become perfect, but I have to say this Step made me see that I deserve to feel pretty good about myself. I have to tell you this Step was a real up for me."

"I thought the crises and conflicts in my life were a result of bad luck and tough breaks or just being in the wrong place or with the wrong person at the wrong time," says Jowin. "I just assumed the mistakes I made were unavoidable or at least understandable, given what I had to deal with at the time. Step Four taught me otherwise. It showed me how my own attitudes and actions shaped my life in predictable, almost inevitable ways. Of course, that applied to the good stuff in my life too. The end result was that I realized the way things turn out has a lot more to do with me than I ever thought it did. For me, the Fourth Step was the most empowering thing I have ever done in my life."

Charlene had been in Al-Anon for years when her husband died. "I was on my own," she explains. "I had to support myself for the first time in my life. It was hell. I blamed my parents, both of whom had been dead for almost twenty years, for not sending me to college. I blamed my husband for making me a stay-at-home wife and not leaving enough money. When I did the Fourth Step, I could see how I had run from financial responsibility all my life. I wanted to be dependent on other people. I wasn't the victim I thought I was. I had been a very willing volunteer."

"I did a Fourth Step the first year I was in recovery," says Robert. "It was about thirty years ago and I was in my thirties.

Once was enough, believe me. But after my slip last year, my new sponsor wanted me to do another. He said he wouldn't sponsor me if I didn't. My inventory was mostly about how useless I felt in retirement. When I saw that, I started doing volunteer work in town. Now I feel more useful than I ever did before!"

"The most distressing thing that got to me with the Fourth Step is the way I lied to my wife about losing our retirement money," says Mack. "Sometimes I told myself I was lying to protect her. I was lying to myself. I didn't want to face the consequences of my actions."

"I didn't realize what a vindictive woman I had become," says Judy, "until I did this Step. As I worked on the Step, it was more about my ex-husband and his new wife than it was about me. What's amazing is that the last ten years of our marriage, I wasn't in love with him. For me, the Fourth Step was a step out of my obsession with a marriage that was over a long time ago. The Fourth Step really helped me move on."

"What was amazing, of course, was how much I had changed," says Charlene. "I see the people in Al-Anon around me changing, especially at the beginning, of course. But I don't notice it so much in myself, especially as I get older. The changes that are happening to me are mostly internal. I'm not so needy anymore. I love my family and my friends, but I don't need them to validate me. That's something that started to come to me with the Fourth Step."

"I remember my sponsor asking me, 'Do you want to be right, or do you want to be happy?'" says Hector. "My answer was I wanted to be right. Frankly, I didn't see the difference. If I wasn't right, how could I be happy? Now I know what happy feels like, and the Fourth Step had a lot to do with it."

Can we really change? Yes! We see it happening every day in the Twelve Step programs—and Step Four is a major factor in people's transformations. For Boomers on the cusp of major lifestyle changes, the Fourth Step is an important reminder that we are still active, evolving creatures. Along with Steps Five through Seven, it also gives us a proven method for recognizing and clearing out the self-defeating thoughts and behaviors that keep us from fully enjoying and contributing to our relationships with other people, and with our Higher Power.

# STEP FIVE

*"Admitted to God, to ourselves, and to another
human being the exact nature of our wrongs."*

IF YOU'VE BEEN AROUND LONG ENOUGH to apply for Social Security (or start thinking about when to apply for it), it's almost inevitable that you've made some mistakes along your life's path. If you're like most of us, you know that some memories of those misdeeds still have the power to make you cringe and want to crawl into the nearest hole.

If you've done Step Four, some of those mistakes should still be fresh in your mind. What do you plan to do with them? From past experience, you know that no matter how hard you try to forget, they never seem to go away. You also know that rationalizing them and explaining them away won't work either. You may even believe the memories are the punishment you deserve for your misconduct. At your age, though, it's beginning to dawn on you that there are some wounds that even time can't heal.

What if you had a chance to let go of the past once and for all? What if there was a way to deactivate the memories that keep on triggering your embarrassment and remorse? Can't even imagine it? Take a look at Step Five. It could be a major step on the path toward a sense of serenity you never even dreamed of. If you take it and complete the process with Steps Six and Seven, you don't have to take any secrets to the grave.

## Owning Your Past

"I used to tell my therapist all the crap I did," says Judy. "I spent a lot of time and money figuring out why I had done what I did, the people and the circumstances that had set me up for it. It was enormously helpful, but it didn't keep the memories from haunting me. Frankly, I had lived with some bad memories so long that it never occurred to me that someday I might be free of them. Step Five was the beginning of my liberation from them. Finally I was able to let go."

You can't let go of something you don't own. When Judy spoke to her therapist, she was indeed acknowledging mistakes she'd made in her past. But acknowledgment is not the same as ownership. It wasn't until she took Step Five that she actually owned what she had done. Once she owned her past, however, she was able to begin the process of letting go.

It makes perfect sense. Even so, most of us can't help being skeptical. AA cofounder Bill Wilson, who formulated the Twelve Steps, wrote that the Steps could work for anyone—except those who are constitutionally incapable of being honest with themselves. It's not their fault. There are, as he wrote, "such unfortunates." Perhaps, for reasons you may not know or fully understand, personal honesty could even do you harm. If that's the case, it's something to look into before moving along with Step Five.

But being uncomfortable, even extremely so, is not the same as being constitutionally incapable. No one expects you will be completely comfortable as you approach this Step. Speaking honestly about oneself, especially one's wrongs, can be hard. Learning how to speak honestly about yourself is a process. It happens over time. In Step Five, you begin the process. Change your behavior, as they say, and the mind will follow. If you're like most of us, you'll have to try it before you believe.

### Where Do You Start?

Generally, we start by looking over our Fourth Step. But the Fifth Step is not simply the spoken version of the Fourth. Here you will be focusing on your wrongs. Many of us have also found the Fifth Step to be a welcome opportunity to share specific secrets that have troubled us, sometimes for years or even decades. If so, why not start with those?

If something from your distant past still bothers you, this is the time to voice it aloud. In general, however, concentrate on what's going on in your life now, or in your recent past. Use Step Five to stay current with yourself. The focus of this Step is the *nature* of the wrongs we have committed. Do you see patterns? Are there certain sets of circumstances that seem to trigger specific responses? For instance, are you scrupulously honest when it comes to money but chronically dishonest with your mate? Or maybe the other way around? Could you be considerate to your family, but feel justified behaving ruthlessly in business? Do you tend to be somewhat judgmental about other people's sex lives, but have some sexual secrets of your own?

"I would own up to something," says Jowin, "but I never left it at that. I didn't stop until I had pointed out how someone else was responsible for what I did. My wife did not put a gun to my head and force me to see other women. My boss did not threaten to fire me unless I padded my expense account. By focusing on the nature of the wrongdoing, I was able to keep the focus on me."

### The "exact nature of our wrongs"

What does this phrase mean? Let's start with a few questions to help us focus.

> *When it comes to personal relationships, how have you let someone down?*

When Charlene's best friend developed breast cancer, Charlene was devastated. But as her friend's disease grew more serious, Charlene invented one excuse after another not to visit her. Earlier, Charlene's sister had died alone in a hospice, and Charlene had never admitted how guilty she felt about not showing up when her sister needed her most.

*When it comes to money or property, have you stolen?*

Mack went on Medicare when he was sixty-five. But he was still employed and his employer continued his medical insurance. He learned how to "double-dip" for his medical expenses, rationalizing that cheating a large insurance company and the government wasn't the same as "real" cheating. When he did Step Five, he had to admit that theft was theft.

*When it comes to marriage and other domestic partnerships, have you been unfaithful?*

After Jowin retired, he sometimes hit on women, usually somebody at the country club where he played golf. Two of the women were good friends of his wife. Although he didn't know if he should admit it to his wife, he knew he had to admit it to God and his sponsor when he did Step Five.

*Have you acted out of prejudice—racial, ethnic, ageist, or sexist bias?*

When her grandchildren brought an African American friend to her home for a pajama party, Judy discouraged her grandchildren from inviting the girl back again. She was ashamed to admit that she had racist attitudes and even more ashamed to realize she was sending a racist message to her grandchildren.

*What other things have you done, intentionally or unintentionally, that have hurt people?*

Even when he was sober, Hector couldn't keep a secret. Once he told his neighbors about a friend who had a secret credit card to pay for porn and lap dances (so his wife wouldn't find out). His friend was angry about the disclosure, but Hector told him he was being silly and oversensitive.

*Are there areas where you've felt entitled to lie or cheat?*

Olga was born poor. But as she became successful in business, she still felt that her deprived childhood entitled her to continue to overcharge her clients, many of whom were considerably poorer than she was.

*And how about the kids?*

Sally had on more than one occasion threatened to disinherit her youngest child but had no intention of doing so. She had to admit she was using threats to hurt and manipulate her daughter.

## Whom Do You Admit Your Wrongs to First?

Chances are you're the harshest, most judgmental critic of your behavior, so it might be wise to start your Fifth Step as a conversation between you and your Higher Power. If you feel, however, that your Higher Power is a foreboding, frightening presence, then it might be wise to speak first to another person.

Either way, you'll eventually need to choose a person to hear your Fifth Step. In the Twelve Step programs, it's usual for us to tell our Fifth Step to our sponsors, but that's hardly mandatory. What's important is to pick a person you feel safe with. Pick someone who isn't immediately involved in your day-to-day life. Don't pick a mate. Or a best friend. Or a business colleague.

"I asked someone I liked but didn't know all that well," says Jowin. "I knew it wouldn't matter to him one way or the other what I said. That made it easier for me to be honest."

"I asked a minister at a church forty miles from home to hear my Fifth Step," says Hector. "He'd officiated at a wedding I'd been to three years before. I wanted someone who didn't know me and would never know me. It may sound excessive, but that's what I felt comfortable with."

"I picked a woman who had been through a lot of the same stuff I had been through," says Judy. "I knew she would understand. That made it easier for me."

"I asked one of the younger members of my AA group to listen to my Fifth Step," says Mack. "That was a big shift for me. I'd always felt I should do a Fifth Step with someone older. I guess I'm less of an 'ageist' than I used to be."

### Tips from Some Experts

"For me, it was like learning a new language," says Mack. "My sponsor told me to start every sentence with 'I' instead of 'he' or 'she.' That wasn't easy. But it was harder to speak of the nature of my wrongs than the wrongs themselves."

"I admitted that I was a vindictive person," says Judy. "My husband's new wife didn't make me do what I did. The prospect of owning my wrongdoings was scary, but once I started sharing, I felt a real sense of relief."

"I had to get honest about my so-called honesty," says Robert. "I used the truth, or what I said was the truth, as a weapon. I wasn't being honest. I was just being mean and trying to make it look like I wasn't. That was hard to admit."

"I could see I was always manipulating the truth," says Charlene. "It was how I manipulated people. So I had to say in my Fifth Step that I was a manipulative person. I didn't like saying it, especially in regard to how I manipulated my children."

"I felt connected," says Judy. "Not just to the woman I had shared my Fifth Step with. To the rest of the world, I think. I wasn't hiding any more. I was real."

"The world didn't end," says Hector. "I admitted to things I'd never admitted to before. Lightning didn't strike. There wasn't any earthquake. It was a surprise."

"I wasn't as bad as I'd feared, frankly," says Olga. "Knowing someone else had done a lot of things I had done was a comfort. I wasn't alone."

"When I told my sponsor the exact nature of my wrongs, I was also telling myself and my Higher Power," says Charlene. "But after I got home, I had a cup of tea and reflected about what had happened. I felt such a sense of serenity. It was amazing to me."

"I am what I do," says Sally. "If I change how I do things, how I speak to people, how I behave, I will become a different person. Step Five gave me a clear picture of where I could initiate the process of change."

Change is what the Twelve Steps are all about. In the next Steps, you'll learn how to create changes you never thought possible. You'll see that you're never too old to change.

# STEP SIX

*"Were entirely ready to have
God remove all these defects of character."*

ARE WE BEING ASKED TO ATTAIN PERFECTION with this Step? Change is hard for all of us, and becoming perfect would be more than most us could bear. Don't worry. We have nothing to fear here. Step Six is about progress, not perfection.

## When Do We Know We're Ready for Change?

How many times have we told ourselves that we weren't ready to make certain changes in our lives? We'd get around to it eventually, we announced firmly, but when we were reminded that "eventually" was now, we decided that it was too late, or we were too old, or what was the point. And it wasn't hard to find peer support for our languor. After teaching a younger generation (or two, or three) about how to live life, a lot of us may very well feel that *our* way is *the* way. We may also feel that one of the benefits of being older is resting on our laurels, such as they are. Let the kids do the heavy lifting in the personal growth area! Who could blame you for wanting to kick back and relax? You've worked hard enough. It's your time, baby!

The truth is, we're never too old to change. That's always been the case, of course, but now that most of us could live twenty or even thirty years longer than our parents, the motivation to change has never been more compelling. As Mack says, "If I were going to live just another three or four years, I probably wouldn't consider changing. I'd find something else to do with my time! But my doctor says I can expect to live well into my eighties. That's a lot of time to be stuck with a defect I know I could be rid of."

Olga adds, half-jokingly, "When I was growing up, my grandparents ruled. Younger people had to put up with them, no matter how crotchety and difficult they were. Young people today aren't so tolerant. They don't let old people get away with anything!"

"I have to remind myself that overcoming character defects wasn't just a favor I did for other people," says Robert. "It's a gift I give myself. It enhances the quality of my own life."

In other words, it's your time . . . ready or not.

### Are We Willing to Change?

Are we addicted to our character defects? Maybe. Maybe not. But no matter how much we may say we hate our defects, we are often dependent on them, just as alcoholics are dependent on alcohol.

"The first time I did this Step," says Robert, "I was in AA a year or so. I thought well, of course, I want to be rid of all my character defects. I mean, what kind of person wouldn't? But as I got real about them, I realized that there were some defects I wasn't ready to give up. I'm proud. I like comparing myself to others. I don't like talking about my problems. It makes me uncomfortable when someone tries to help me. I don't think I'd ever ask anyone for help. I know I think too much about money. I was surprised, frankly. Once I saw how some of my defects worked against me, I realized I needed to give this Step more serious thought."

For those of us who have not worked the Steps before, this is totally new terrain. But even those of us who, like Robert, have used the Twelve Steps to put down the drink and deal with other issues, can still feel hesitant about letting go of our defects of character.

Many of us have found it helpful to check out the history of our defects: how they got started and how we made them work for us. It may surprise us to see that many of them started out as assets. For some of us, they were actually survival tools. But even when our survival didn't depend on them, we often found that these character defects came in mighty handy.

Olga's anger was the fuel she needed to make her way in the business world. It also turned out to be a useful tool when it came to intimidating colleagues and scaring adversaries. When Mack first heard someone mention "rigorous honesty," he explained he was a used-car dealer and no honest man could make a living at that. Guilt-tripping her ex-husband was the only way Judy could make sure he would come through with the alimony checks.

But that was then. The tools you needed when you were younger may have outlived their usefulness. Can you see how they are actually taking a toll on you and the ones you love?

Ask yourself:

- Do you still enjoy your defects?
- Do you need them?
- How do you use them to get what you want?
- How do they keep you from getting what you want?
- Are you willing to find other, healthier ways to get what you need and what you want in life?

Generally, it's only after we realize the pain our character defects cause for us and the people we love that we are able to ask our Higher Power to remove them. How many alcoholics even consider the possibility of giving up alcohol *before* the law intervenes—or their health, their work, or their family life is in danger? How many people turn to Al-Anon *before* their codependence has made them unhappy enough to consider changing themselves, rather than trying to change the people around them?

But entirely willing doesn't have to mean totally desperate. You don't need to hit rock bottom before you look for a way up.

## Tips from Some Experts

"What made me ready and willing," says Craig, "was a lot of pain. My defects worked for me, or so I thought. My defects got me the attention I craved. They also helped me get rid of the people I didn't want in my life. It wasn't until I got sober that I realized that my defects weren't working for me. That's what made me willing."

"It's not as though I didn't know I had a defect or two, but I kind of figured they were here to stay," Mack says. "I kind of figured they were part of me. I used to laugh about it: how would my kids recognize me if I didn't have my defects on? Besides, I was used to the extra money I was making from my insurance scam. Frankly, I didn't know how I was going to make ends meet without the money. It wasn't such an easy decision."

Was Sally ready to give up volunteering to be her father's sole caretaker?

"I knew I'd been stuck in that role most of my life, and I knew that I had to make a change and I had to do it while he was still alive. I guess it was his mortality that made me decide I was ready to give it up."

How willing was Mack to admit to lying to his wife about their economic situation?

"I wasn't ready," he says. "Not right away. If I told my wife what was going on, I knew she'd be hurt and there would be consequences I didn't want to pay."

Jowin knew he had to stop cheating on his wife from his Fourth Step. Jowin also knew that he was infantilizing his children. He knew that he was enabling them by supporting them as he did, by letting his son live with him, and by sometimes even paying off his son's debts. But being able to help his kids made him feel good about himself. If he stopped enabling them, he would have to be prepared for their reaction. He would need to find other ways to feel good about himself.

As ashamed as Charlene was about not being there for her dying sister, she still doubted that she would ever have the courage to see anyone through the last stage of life. When she opened up to a friend about it, she found that others knew just how she felt. They had learned to be brave by finding various ways to be useful to people who were terminally ill. Charlene realized she could do it too—if only she were prepared to devote time and energy to it.

It's not a matter of IQ, education, income, health. If you're willing, then you're able.

Not all the women and men in our group of experts were willing to have God remove all their defects of character. Most of them chose instead to focus on one or two at a time. Some weren't sure they were "entirely" willing, but decided to give it their best shot anyway . . . as you'll see in the following Steps.

Bill Wilson wrote that sobriety requires the willingness to go to any lengths. "Any lengths" may mean one thing to one person and something quite different to another. But it's clear that we become who we are only if we make a conscientious, concentrated effort to change. Remember, you will not be removing your defects all by yourself. Your Higher Power will be doing the job for you. Don't believe it? Then read on. Learning to believe is what Step Seven is all about.

# STEP SEVEN

*"Humbly asked Him to remove our shortcomings."*

THE TWELVE STEPS ARE ALL ABOUT CHANGE. For Baby Boomers, change has gained a meaning it didn't have for us earlier. Many of us have, albeit reluctantly, come to realize that after a lifetime of trying to change the people, places, and things around us, the only kind of real change can come from within. Sometimes that comes after a total failure at changing others. But even when we succeeded, when we managed to exert some degree of control over the world around us, we still didn't feel the contentment we had sought.

## A Midpoint Review

Now that you are midway through the Steps, it's a good time to take a look at how far you have come. It will also give you a chance to get some fresh perspective as you launch into the remaining Steps. Has it been harder than you imagined? Easier? Any major surprises? How have you benefited from the Steps so far? Be honest here. If it's not working for you, it's time to take a serious look. Remember that Twelve-Steppers work by attraction, not promotion. No one's going to be on your case if this is not your cup of tea.

At first glance, it may have seemed that some Steps would be a challenge and others might be a snap. That may have turned out to be the case, but by now it should be clear that every one of the Twelve Steps is important, though some may seem more significant than others the first or even the second time around.

Some of them may have seemed especially challenging, even unpleasant. The Fourth Step stands out for most of us—not many people enjoy facing up to their character flaws. But we know that it's do-able, no matter how little we actually want to do it. Others, like Step One, may not seem to make sense the first time we grapple with the idea of powerlessness. Of course, it's the "God thing" in Step Three that provokes the most bewilderment, confusion, and skepticism for many of us. But as we worked this Step, we found a new serenity and freedom in finally being able to trust in the God of our understanding.

What we have (hopefully) learned in the first Steps is that exercising our will does not make our lives better. We also learned that many of the coping skills we were taught as we grew up have also failed us. A number of them have actually turned out to be self-defeating behaviors resulting from the very character defects that tend to make our lives unbearable—or at least certain aspects of our lives.

## Step Seven Asks Us to Get Out of the Way

As we become more accustomed to looking inward rather than pointing outward, we are more willing, even eager, to change ourselves in profound ways. The key is to get out of the way and let it happen. Step Seven is a major, conscious attempt to invite a benevolent, caring Higher Power to help us. That's harder than it may seem at first. Asking for help is not what the stereotypical Boomer is all about. Those Boomers in fact are living proof that humility doesn't necessarily come with age. "We're the guys who can do it on our own, thank you."

"When I get lost in my car," laughs Robert, "I'm not better about asking someone for directions now than I ever was. In fact, I'm worse. Everyone's getting so young, and I hate looking like a stupid old man."

"I was always asking for help," says Sally. "But I did it to ingratiate myself with people. I knew it made people feel good about them. It was part of my people pleasing."

"Humility was getting harder for me," says Mack. "I was a

regular know-it-all, and arrogantly justifying it as one of the prerogatives of my senior status at work and with my family."

Says Hector, "I was always an obstinate guy, and age had only made me more so. But someone explained to me that being humble meant being teachable. That made me think."

"I was in the program five years before I did this Step," says Olga. "I was thinking therapy would remove my shortcomings. I thought they would disappear in time. They didn't. I prayed a lot. That brought me some peace of mind, but it didn't solve the problem. I took this Step only when everything else failed. Step Seven was a last resort."

"I took my Sixth Step list of defects and I prayed," says Judy. "I spent an afternoon humbly asking my Higher Power to take away my defects. I could hardly believe this was actually happening to me. The next morning I felt so incredible. By the end of the day, however, I had lost my temper at work, I'd worked up a major resentment over my husband's new wife, and I'd lied to someone at the cable TV company. It was clear to me my defects were still very much with me."

### Our Higher Power's Timetable

Contrary to what we may have inferred, shortcomings are not removed instantaneously. In fact, expecting them to be removed and feeling disappointed, even a little cheated, when they are not, shows that you have indeed overlooked—or chosen to ignore—the word "humbly" here. Humility doesn't come easily. Nor does the belief that any power, no matter how high, could actually remove our defects. But belief in this Step comes with practice, and with practice, the genuine humility and surrender that are at the heart of the Seventh Step will come.

Our Higher Power usually works on its own timetable, not

ours. One day at a time, as we become more willing to let go of our shortcomings, as we ask our Higher Power to remove them, we come to know that this Step is for real. It's a process. The first stage is almost always where we learn that there's a difference between a feeling and a fact. We have learned it's not the feelings that are our shortcoming. Feelings are feelings. They are neither good nor bad, right nor wrong. The shortcoming may have to do with how we act on our feelings. Too often, however, we have assumed that the feeling was a fact. If we felt like a drink, we had a drink. If we felt angry, we hit. If we felt hurt, we were too quick to retaliate.

But with time, we become more accustomed to distinguishing the fact from the feeling. Just because we feel like a drink doesn't mean we have to have one. We do other things instead— go to a meeting, call a sponsor, pray. The same applies when we have those feelings that can lead to damaging behavior. We go back to the Steps. We use the tools that have proved so effective to Twelve-Steppers for more than seven decades.

As we change our behavior, we almost invariably find that the feelings themselves dissipate, coming up less often and less powerfully. We have, in effect, remapped our brains—and that is literally true, according to recent scientific evidence on how behavior changes brain chemistry. Yes, it's true that we take it one day at a time, but as we put five, ten, or fifteen years of recovery under our belts, we gain confidence in our ability to refrain from drinking, drugging, or engaging in other self-defeating addictive behaviors.

## Teachability and Willingness to Change

Not all resistance to being teachable comes from arrogance. A lot of it can be fear-based as well. How many of us have felt totally baffled by the new technologies? How many people over fifty have figured out how to program their DVD player? Hector is not alone when he says he still hasn't figured out how to send text messages . . . and he's had a cell phone for almost eight years. "I got embarrassed asking my nephew to explain it to me."

Is it possible to be too old to learn? Even if you haven't actually been thinking that, you may have been acting like it. You may also have developed a defensive manner that suggests you already know everything you need to know in life. We are bound to know a lot just by virtue of having lived a number of years. But when it comes to facing the many challenges of aging, we are only just beginning.

## One Shortcoming at a Time

Although most, if not all, of us entertain the possibility of having all our shortcomings removed at once, it's more usual for us to take the Seventh Step one shortcoming at a time.

Are any of the following people's shortcomings familiar to you?

Laziness: "After working hard for forty years," says Hector, "I was looking forward to a lot of time off. I deserved a rest. What happened was I became a couch potato. This was not getting a rest. This was total slothdom."

Isolation: "Before, I had my family to take care of. My kids. I had a whole community I pretty much had to socialize with," says Sally. "I was looking forward to spending a little time with myself. It wasn't a year before I realized I had cut off ties with just about everyone I could."

Vanity: "I wish I had learned to give up being so vain," says Judy. "I guess I've wanted to look like I was twenty-three from the time I was about six. And when I got to be twenty-three, I wanted to stay that way forever. I asked for God to remove the part of my vanity that was turning my life into a series of cosmetic surgeries. Now, thanks to the Seventh Step, I just want to look the best I can for someone my age, although people do say I look ten years younger."

Stinginess: "Granted, we're all worried about money," says Hector. "But I became a miser. Just as bad, I never shut up about how tight money was. It got to be people were even avoiding me because of all my talk about money."

Ageism: "I find myself going back and forth between how superior older people are or how inferior we are," says Hector. "I don't know which is worse, but it's clear to me that both are having a pretty negative effect on my life."

Worry and fear: "I worried so much about being sick that I made myself sick," says Jowin. "I started having cancer scares of my own making every six months. I guess it was really a case of self-centered fear."

"I was afraid of being poor," says Olga. "I justified it by explaining to everyone that my family was very poor. That's true, but I know I'm inclined to see the glass as being completely empty. It's almost like an addiction to my own negativity."

"Death," says Sally. "There's a lot going around these days, and it's getting closer. Now that my mom and her sister are gone, I realize there is no barrier generation between me and the grim reaper. When I came to see that as more about me than about death itself, I was able to bring it to my Seventh Step. It worked too. It made me a believer, actually."

"Old age," Craig says. "I was diagnosed with HIV about twenty years ago. I always figured I would die of AIDS. So I didn't save money for my old age. I wasn't going to have one! Now it looks like I will, especially now that I'm off drugs. So now instead of worrying about death, which I can handle, I'm worrying about old age. Thanks to Step Seven, I'm doing something about my old age instead of fretting about it."

Once a shortcoming is lifted, will it be forever? Yes, it can be if we remain humble. "I got cocky about my sobriety," says Robert. "I'd been sober so long I thought I had outgrown my addiction to liquor. Despite all the disastrous things I ever heard from men and women who had gone back to drinking, I thought it wouldn't happen to me. Now I know why so many people in AA call themselves 'recovering alcoholics' rather than 'recovered alcoholics.'"

Ask people who learned to control their anger or their resentment or their lust—or their whatever—if they have stopped having those feelings altogether. Most of them will assure you that they still have the feelings, but they'll add that the longer they've controlled their actions, the easier it is to manage their feelings.

## Tips from Some Experts

"I say the Seventh Step prayer every morning," says Sally (see page 115). "That's a big help in keeping mindful of the proclivity I have for obsessing about death."

"I'm going to more AA meetings," says Robert. "I'm doing service again. That helps me stay humble, and that in turn keeps me away from the drink."

"When I start itching for more plastic surgery, I do the Second Step," says Judy, "just to remind myself I'm nuts. Then I go to Step Seven. So far it's worked like a charm."

"I do Step One before I do Seven," says Jowin. "It's good to remind myself of my powerlessness and also of how unmanageable my shortcomings make my life."

"It works," says Olga. "That's the amazing thing. Even after all these years of working Step Seven, I remained amazed. My sponsor says that's my humility showing. I would say that this is the Step that taught me how to be humble."

With the humility that we gain from Steps Four through Seven, we are ready to tackle the remaining "Action Steps": Eight through Twelve.

*"Made a list of all persons we had harmed, and became
willing to make amends to them all."*

"THERE ARE NO VICTIMS; just volunteers."

Anyone around in the 1980s probably remembers hearing that slogan. If you were in one of the Twelve Step programs, more than likely you heard it time and time again. It was meant, no doubt, to encourage self-empowerment. It was supposed to remind us that we have choices.

But the truth of the matter is that some people *are* victims, not volunteers.

Getting real about ways we have been victimized can be an important aspect of anyone's recovery. That can be a key part of Step Four. But when we come to Step Eight, it's time to focus on *our* victims. Okay, so maybe some of them were unduly vulnerable. There are certainly some people who seem to make a habit, even a lifestyle, of being in the wrong place at the wrong time. If adversity doesn't wipe you out, it makes you stronger—or that's what we're told. No doubt you've heard someone on TV, or at a meeting, or even a friend say, "It turned out that going bankrupt was the best thing that ever happened to me." Or maybe it was getting sick, being left by a mate, or some other misfortune: just fill in the blank.

Most of us have talked about how adversity in one form or another has shaped our character, how it's hurt and damaged us, how we've coped and persevered. Nowadays, though, it seems that talking about the bad things that have happened to us and the people who mess with us has become a social mainstay. It's how many people ingratiate themselves with their friends.

All of this is well and good, but none of it is really relevant when we're working this Step. Now's the time to take a look at how *we* have harmed other people. Even if they were volunteer victims—and no doubt some of them were—they were still *our* victims.

In the past, when we've looked at how we've harmed others,

we've employed some defense to defuse the hurt. How often have we offered a self-serving explanation to go along with our acknowledgment that we have hurt someone? We all have ways of copping a plea on this one. Do any of the following sound familiar?

"There were circumstances beyond my control!"

"Actually, it was my mother who made me do it (or my wife, my business colleague: fill in the blank)."

"Yes, I did it but I had no idea it would hurt him (her, them)."

"I meant well."

"I'm just a lousy mate (or parent, or friend). Whoever I've harmed should have known better than to expect otherwise from me."

"I was drinking and I didn't know what I was doing."

"It was honestly the best I could do at the time, and though I knew it wasn't right, I thought it was better than doing nothing."

"Honest, I didn't know she was your best friend."

Feel free to add your own variations on the theme. No matter how good these kinds of excuses sounded at the time, or even now, remember that none of it makes any difference when you write your list. No matter what you meant or what the context, regardless of what anyone may have done to precipitate your action, the name of the person who was harmed goes on the list. If you were on a tear or off your meds, it makes no difference. Morally and ethically, maybe even legally, you may not be responsible, but if you want to do this Step the way it was originally intended, you are accountable.

## Holding Yourself Accountable

Accountability is what Step Eight comes down to. What's key to remember here is that it's a preparatory list. While this Step is also about becoming ready to make amends, it's not about making amends—not yet. That's Step Nine, and in any case you probably shouldn't start making amends with anyone on your list until you have discussed the list with another person. You may find when you come to the Ninth Step that you need to make some deletions as well as some additions. And how you go about making your amends is also something you'll want to discuss with a sponsor or trusted friend. We'll address that in more detail when we get to that Step. For now, let's just focus on making the list.

The key to the Eighth Step is the willingness to look at yourself in a way that may be entirely new to you. As with the Fourth Step, it's about looking at yourself honestly and critically, without beating up on yourself. It's also about focusing on your life as a series of choices you have made. Working the Twelve Steps is all about acknowledging you have more choices than you imagined. Learning that much of the grief you have faced in life is a direct or indirect result of bad choices, rather than bad luck, is a key to genuinely empowering yourself. Although losing some illusions and delusions about your blamelessness can make you feel vulnerable, like you're losing your innocence, you will gain so much more. "Owning your stuff" can put you back in control of your life in ways you won't fully understand until you experience it.

## Tips from Some Experts

"I was in my fifties when I came to this Step for the first time," says Jowin. "That's a heap of living. Frankly, I didn't know where to begin. My sponsor suggested I start with my Fourth Step. As I looked it over, I started to write out names. Just names. One after another. Must have been fifteen in all. I didn't go into details about the things I did that harm them. I just stayed with the list. That was all I needed to do at that point."

"I'm in my sixties," says Judy. "I started my list with the people I hated the most, the ones who I felt had wronged me the most. That meant my husband and his new wife. I didn't feel sorry for them or apologetic for what I'd done, but the Step doesn't say you have to feel sorry, does it?"

"I guess it's hurting the kids that's the hardest part," says Mack. "It's always been a thorn in my side, knowing I wasn't as good a dad as they deserved. But I'd always been kind of vague about the damage I'd done to them. I was always saying I did the best I could, given the circumstances. When I did this Step, I had to focus on my actions instead of the circumstances."

"My parents always felt so guilty about me," says Craig. "I used to tell them my drinking and drugging had nothing to do with them, but the truth is I really believed it did. They worried that somehow they were responsible for me being gay, and they thought that was why I drank. I know now they didn't make me gay any more than being gay made me drink. But once I got sober, I knew I'd liked guilt-tripping them. It was hard to face, but I had to admit that I had harmed them."

"I had to admit that my disciplining my kids bordered on abuse," says Charlene. "Sometimes I felt so helpless, so angry. I just couldn't control my feelings. I liked spanking them. I didn't feel good till they started crying."

"If you kill someone," says Robert, "it's pretty clear how you've harmed them. The same applies if you robbed someone, or burned his or her house down. If you've abused someone physically, that should be clear too, even though it's tough to face that. But what about the harm we do when we lie to someone? What about the harm we do when we manipulate them? What about invading their privacy?"

"I cheated on my wife," says Jowin. "Even though she never found out the specifics, she sensed something was wrong. Now I can see how it undermined her confidence. Not just in me, which is totally understandable, but in herself, which is also understandable, but it took me a while to get it."

"I'm a terrific procrastinator," says Olga. "I'm late for everything. It got so that I was pathological. But it's like my drinking. I kept telling myself the only one who was getting hurt was me. I knew it irritated people, but I couldn't help it. That's what I told myself anyway, and maybe at the time it was true. But irritating people is harming them. When you make people wait on you, it's robbing them of their time. It's showing how you don't respect them. As I make my list, I try to be mindful of what I have done and what actual harm it may have done to them. I know when someone lies to me, invades my privacy, keeps me waiting. All too often, it confirms my worst fears about themselves. It can undermine my confidence."

Robert G. puts it this way. "Since I retired, I've become addicted to true crime cases. One thing that always gets me is when the defendant admits he's guilty. I can't believe how often it goes something like, 'I'd like to apologize for any harm I might have caused.' *Might* have caused? He's got to be kidding! He killed someone! But it got me thinking how most people, myself included, issue our apologies with a caveat. The Eighth Step has been major in helping me acknowledge that it's not a matter of 'if' I did damage: in fact, I did damage. Step Nine shows me how to repair the damage I did."

Start by looking at your track record so far with acknowledging the harm you may have done others in the past and identifying your shortcomings as you fully admit your wrongs. Then take a look at the people who showed up in your Fourth Step and add anyone you've thought about since then, perhaps ones who've come to mind as you read this chapter. Once your list is finished, you're ready for the Ninth Step.

## STEP NINE

*"Made direct amends to such people
wherever possible, except when to do so would
injure them or others."*

SAYS OLGA, "I DREADED THIS STEP. But it taught me old dogs can learn new tricks, and that was something that made me very glad. I didn't feel so helpless any more. I had no idea how liberating this would be for me!"

Step Nine is an action step. It may sound like more action than most of us are prepared for! In the other Steps, if you were talking to anyone, it was to God or to your sponsor or whoever listened to your Fifth Step. While you may have dreaded taking the action before, you knew that both God and your sponsor were rooting for you. This time you may be taking a chance with someone who may not be in your corner.

## Amends Are More Than Apologies

The first thing to do is to realize that we're not talking apologies. Apologies, for many of us, both giving and receiving, can come cheap.

How many times over the years do alcoholics and other addicts say they're sorry? And how many times do they actually mean it? The experts from our sample group recall some of the habitual apologies they made before they started working the Steps—and the motives behind the apologies.

"I used to apologize to my children for being sick," says Judy.

"I apologized to my kids for not making better money," says Jowin.

"I used to tell my husband I was sorry that my breasts weren't bigger," says Sally. "How pathetic is that?"

"I used to apologize for the weather if it rained when we were having a picnic," says Hector.

"I apologized to my wife for anything, all the time, because basically she never shut up until I did," says Mack.

"I used to apologize if the movie I picked was bad," says Robert.

"When my husband got drunk, he'd break things," says Charlene. "I'd apologize for making him do it. Sometimes I'd even apologize for having done it."

More than likely, we could add some examples of our own. Some of them, like Charlene's, would be poignant, no doubt. Some of them would be funny, like Hector's apology for the weather. Sometimes we apologized to appease and other times to manipulate. How many times have we apologized for one wrong in order to avoid being scrutinized for a more important offense? The motives might vary, but one fact is consistent: these kinds of apologies are mostly baseless and accomplish little but perpetuate our problems.

So while the first few words you may be saying to one of the men, women, or children on your Eighth Step list may be "I'm sorry" or "I want to apologize," let's be clear from the start: Step Nine is not really about making apologies. It's about making amends, clearing up the wreckage of our past so that we can get rid of the fears and resentments that threaten our serenity and could eventually lead to relapse.

### Review Your List Before You Start Making Amends

For most of us, before we start actually contacting the people on our list, we should go over it with a trusted friend or sponsor. But even before you speak with that person, prepare for the discussion by considering the questions listed below. You'll be in a better position to receive guidance on getting started making your amends.

- Which amends are most pressing?
- For each situation, what would be the best way to approach that person? In person? (This is the most effective if at all possible.) By phone? By email or letter?
- How much time are you willing to spend to make amends?
- If you're making financial amends, are you willing to make full restitution right away? If not, do you have a plan for paying the person back?
- If you're making amends that involve a change in your behavior, what are you willing to do to make restitution?
- Are there people on your list who would be harmed if you made direct amends? In what way? What can you do instead?
- What do you plan to do about the people who are no longer physically available for direct amends?

"I was inclined to do it in passing," says Judy. "Sort of, 'Oh, by the way . . .' I'd catch my breath during the anxious pause that followed and then change the subject as quickly as I could. My sponsor told me I had to be a whole lot more out-there. I had to call up the first person on my list, make a date to get together. Not at a restaurant or a movie. I invited her to my home. When she got there and I'd served her tea, I told her I wanted to make amends for what I had done. I was so nervous. But the minute I started, a terrific sense of tranquility came over me."

"Face to face is best," says Hector. "But I was afraid of making amends to my sister in person. To tell you the truth, I'd always been afraid of her. Even though she's almost seventy now, I'm still anxious when I'm with her. I wrote her a letter. She told me she got it. She told me I tortured myself unnecessarily. That was it. I felt kind of like she was dismissing me, and I guess she was. I wish I had done it in person, but the letter was the best I could do."

"It was the financial amends that were the ones I had to start with," says Craig. "I borrowed money from my parents all the time. They even went into their retirement accounts to bail me out, and I never paid the money back. Frankly, I never really meant to pay them back. I thought they owed me for my rotten childhood. Besides, I was going to get the money anyway in the end when they died.

"I was in the hole when I finally started going to CMA meetings. There was no way in the world I could imagine paying them anything back. But my sponsor suggested I make a plan. A certain amount every week. It wasn't much, but I'm sticking to it. It's been two years, and I still haven't made much of dent in the debt I owe, but I'm changing inside. That's making amends, isn't it?"

"My problem was the same, but the opposite," says Mack. "I took money from my kids' college funds. My kids wound up working their way through college. If it weren't for the student loans, they wouldn't have made it. When I got sober, I took over some of the loans."

"I used money to manipulate my kids," says Charlene. "The money situation wasn't the best at our house, but I always had the next month's rent and more than enough for food and medical. But I was always acting like we were on the brink of financial extinction, and that seemed to keep them in line. It was kind of like I was giving them a false sense if insecurity. It helped them to hear me talk about it later. Hearing them talk about it was painful, but I knew part of my amends was listening for as long as they wanted to talk."

Not all parental amends are financial, of course. Some are emotional. "I had to make amends to my kids," says Robert. "I took care of them financially, but the fact was I resented them. I did what I thought was being responsible, but I was distant. I didn't abuse them, but I know they were afraid. How do you make amends for that? They were grown. I told my sponsor I thought it was too late. My sponsor told me that it was never too late. So what I did was to tell them how I felt as a young father and how I think it deprived them of the loving feelings they deserved. I made it clear that it was me, it wasn't them."

Sometimes what's broken, though, cannot be repaired. That certainly is the case with child abuse. Making amends for abuse, emotional or physical, to children (or adults, for that matter) can be the most challenging of all. Although there's no way to undo the damage, the parent's acknowledgment of the damage done and an expression of responsibility and remorse can be an enormous help in the survivor's own healing. Again, discuss it fully beforehand with someone else, perhaps even a professional, especially if there are legal ramifications.

Some parents overcompensate at times, and that can lead to problems.

Says Jowin, "When my children grew up, I was doing pretty well financially. I indulged them. I stopped paying my son's gambling debts, but my daughter as an adult was totally dependent on me. I guess it massaged my ego. I wasn't a bad dad anymore. But I was also enabling her. She never managed to live on her income. So I was subsidizing her. When she had trouble with relationships, I always assured her she was right and everyone else was wrong. When I did my Ninth Step, I talked to her about it. I told her I need to change that. She was angry. I was expecting her to be upset, but I just wasn't prepared for how mad she'd be. She's still not talking to me. I was kind of expecting that. I hope it'll pass, but I knew I was doing the right thing for her and for me."

## Some Amends Can't Be Made Directly

There may be amends on our list that we are not ready to make yet. Sometimes that's because of ongoing resentments and issues that have yet to be resolved.

"I did some things I'm not proud of to my husband's new wife," says Judy. "I haven't actually made my amends to her, but I do realize it is something I really want to do . . . eventually."

"I know I should make financial restitution to my former employers," says Jowin. "But they overworked me, so I felt totally justified in padding my expense account. I think I'd resent giving the money back. My sponsor says I should just sit with it. Pray. The right answer will come to me in time, he says."

"My brother-in-law was on the list," says Olga. "I thought I owed him amends over a dispute that arose when my sister's will went to probate. When I talked it over with a friend, however, my friend pointed out it was really my brother-in-law who owed me amends, not that he was ever going to make them."

Some amends must be silent, especially if they would harm others. "I decided it would be self-serving of me to tell my wife about the other women I'd been seeing," says Jowin. "It would hurt more than I can say. For the longest time, I blamed her for being difficult and cold, but that was just my way of justifying my liaisons. Now that I'm warmer and affectionate with her, and not feeling guilty, she's become a lot warmer too." (Jowin's decision may have been right for his situation. But think seriously where infidelity is concerned, and remember your responsibility to communicate about possible sexually transmitted diseases.)

"I couldn't make amends to one of my children," says Charlene. "He died of an overdose just a couple months after I had started in Al-Anon. I wrote him a letter, though. A very long, detailed one. I really poured my heart into it. I had a little ceremony where I burned the letter and released it into the cosmos. I'm very conscious now that I treat my grandkids the way I wish I had treated my son. That's my way of making amends."

Sometimes we are not ready to make amends because the consequences are too daunting.

"Don't forget the last words here: '. . . except when to do so would injure them or others,'" says Robert. "I read about one Twelve-Stepper who went to trial when he wrote an amends letter to a girl he'd date raped twenty years ago. How many of us would be willing to do jail time? I have to say he didn't seem to regret making the amends, though."

"One of my sponsees was a nurse who'd stolen drugs from the hospital," says Charlene. "If she made direct amends, she might have lost her job and had her license suspended. She has children to support. She felt she couldn't do it to them. She felt her children were among the others whom it might have harmed."

"If I had made financial amends for double-dipping," says Mack, "I would have been liable to a lawsuit, and I couldn't put my family in that kind of economic jeopardy. But I have changed my behavior. I don't do anything in my life now that could get me into that kind of trouble. So I have changed, and that's making amends, isn't it?"

"I had to make amends to my daughter-in-law," says Sally. "I dislike her, but I had no right telling her she didn't know the first thing about raising kids. While I was talking to her, she acted like she wasn't listening. At one point she even turned up the volume on the TV set. But I stuck with it. If anything, I like her even less than I did before I started to make amends, but I feel that whatever unfinished business there was between us is finished now. You know how there are some people you just feel you've got to get the last word with? That's how I felt, but now I don't. I don't have to go there ever again."

Although most amends bring positive responses from the people we are making amends to, we need to be prepared, as Sally was, for negative responses. We need to let the people we are making amends to have their say too, and it may not be pretty. Some will want to tell their side of the story. Some may even feel the need to do your personal inventory. They may ascribe motives to you that were never true. They may tell you the damage was even worse than you had imagined. Occasionally, it will signal the end of a friendship. We need to be prepared for that.

## The Payoff

But even when we try to make amends and it goes badly, we come away knowing it was the right thing to do. For the other person. For ourselves. So often we feel fear, anxiety, embarrassment, and shame going into this Step, but coming out of it, how different we feel. There's usually a new sense of calm that we haven't felt before, a kind of relief. While we most likely feel humbled, it's unlikely that we'll feel humiliated. Instead of feeling too small or too big, we feel "right-sized" at last.

"What surprised me most," says Charlene, "is how it raised the bar on my relationships. The good ones got better. The not-so-good ones began to fade—not in anger or resentment. It was just that I was evolving to a whole new level, and some of my relationships seemed to be stuck—and seemed to be okay with staying that way."

As we worked the first eight Steps, we made dramatic changes in our thinking and in our behavior. As we take this Step, we are making a dramatic, conscious change in our behavior with the people in our lives. We are acting in far healthier, more considerate ways than ever before. In making amends, we are learning responsible ways to handle family, friends, employers—all the important people in our lives.

"It cleaned the slate," says Olga. "I still have baggage, but it weighs one-tenth of what it used to."

"It showed me that I don't have to behave as either a bully or a doormat in my relationships," says Mack.

"In the AA Big Book," says Robert, "there's a list of twelve promises that will come true if you follow the Steps. They have to do with being more comfortable with yourself, more confident in your dealings with other people, with money, more hopeful about the future. These promises come right after the Ninth Step. That's not surprising for anyone who has been there and done them."

*If we are painstaking about this phase of our development, we will be amazed before we are half way through. We are going to know a new freedom and a new happiness. We will not regret the past nor wish to shut the door on it. We will comprehend the word serenity and we will know peace. No matter how far down the scale we have gone, we will see how our experience can benefit others. That feeling of uselessness and self-pity will disappear. We will lose interest in selfish things and gain interest in our fellows. Self-seeking will slip away. Our whole attitude and outlook upon life will change. Fear of people and of economic insecurity will leave us. We will intuitively know how to handle situations which used to baffle us. We will suddenly realize that God is doing for us what we could not do for ourselves.\**

*The promises are taken from *Alcoholics Anonymous,* 4th ed., published by AA World Services, Inc., New York, NY, 83–84.

"As I embark on the next stage of my life," says Judy, "it's incredible to know that my life can be more productive, more connected, and just a lot happier than I could have ever imagined. I was sixty when I did this Step for the first time. Really, I felt my life was just beginning. It's exciting. I never imagined I'd feel this way. My life did begin at sixty, thanks to this Step."

# STEP TEN

*"Continued to take personal inventory and when we were wrong promptly admitted it."*

REMEMBER THOSE GROUCHY, perennially malcontented old codgers from your childhood, fifty—or more!—years ago? If they were next-door neighbors, you made sure to stay out of their yard, turn the radio down, and never let the dog even look at their lawn—or you'd never hear the end of it. If the codgers were family, you had to sleep on the couch downstairs so they could use your room when they visited—and not once did they stop complaining.

Remember how they never had a kind thing to say about anyone or anything? They shook their collective heads at the clothes today, the kids today, the music today, the cost of everything. All they ever talked about was how good movies used to be and how well-mannered kids were when they were growing up. According to them, the world was going down the tubes. Who could have blamed you for sighing with relief when those tiresome codgers moved away or went back home?

The good news is that those old grouches have moved on to a much happier place, one where no one is ever grouchy. The bad news is that there's another generation just now getting ready to take their place. If you listen carefully, you can hear some of them warming up in the wings, complaining and grumbling. Don't be surprised if some of them are your friends. You could be married to one of them. In fact, *you* could be one of them! Yes, it's the Boomers. Us. You and me. No, it's not inevitable. It's a choice, though too many of us are making it unconsciously. If you see yourself here, you *can* opt out, but you must act immediately. Work the Tenth Step and you, too, can avoid morphing into a grumpy old man or woman—one day at a time.

## A Maintenance Step

Step Ten is the first of what are generally referred to as the maintenance steps. It's about living in the present. As we age, we seem to become more focused on our past than we are on today. Getting together with friends to reminisce can help keep bonds strong. Scrapbooking, watching an old movie, returning to the places where we grew up—these are healthy, life-affirming things to do. But when we start to dwell too much on yesterday, we lose today. Grumpy old seniorhood is often the consequence. We may complain about being marginalized by younger people, but the truth is we may be marginalizing ourselves.

"It's funny how little things can get so out of proportion," says Mack. "Especially if your mind works like mine does. I realized when I did my Fourth Step what a resentful guy I was. I mean, I can nurse a small slight into an apocalypse. Step Ten is my way of making sure that World War III doesn't break out in my head. Every evening, usually just before I sit down to dinner, I go over the day. I make a mental list of the people who pissed me off."

"I used to think that if I acknowledged my feelings, then I would be a slave to them," says Olga. "It turned out it was just the opposite. I'm a slave to the feelings I don't acknowledge. It wasn't the first time I had it exactly wrong."

"The Tenth Step helps me detect problem areas that I only started to recognize when I took my Fourth Step," says Craig. "I'm always waiting for someone else to take care of my problems. I saw that very clearly in my Fourth Step. When I do Step Ten, I can see how I'm doing it again."

"I know I overreact to certain things," Craig adds. "I'm too quick to feel people don't like me. In the past, if someone seemed to be ignoring me, I assumed it was all about me. It never occurred to me that they had their own problems. Now, when I do my Tenth Step, I try to be especially mindful to when I'm feeling hurt, I remind myself it's just a feeling. No one hurt me. It's made a big difference."

"I'm an over-eater," says Sally. "It's been a long time since I acted out with food. But what I need to do is watch out for those 'drink signals.' That's what I focus on when I do my Tenth Step. Do I feel resentful? Do I feel afraid or impotent? Do I need to go to more meetings? When my sponsor moved to Florida, I didn't bother to get a new one. I realized when I was doing my Tenth Step that even though I have been in the program for years, I still need a sponsor."

Mack adds, "My sponsor told me that it almost never happens that a crisis lasts more than four hours. That means enough time to call the police or get to the hospital. Even military battles rarely last more than four hours. That was a revelation to me. When I do the Tenth Step, I'm amazed that the crises were all in my mind, or my kids' minds."

Sometimes the Tenth Step can help promote other healthier behaviors:

"I have a tough time standing up for myself," says Charlene. "Yesterday it was a girlfriend who still owes me fifteen bucks. I hated bringing it up, but fifteen bucks is fifteen bucks. It's awkward mentioning it. I feel petty. I know she thinks I'm being petty. But I know how I am and how I get. So I took an action and reminded her. I know it's better for me to be embarrassed than to feel resentful."

"I get lonely," says Robert. "I hate admitting it to myself. Probably because I hate making telephone calls, making dates. But when I'm feeling down, I check out that feeling. Once I recognize the feeling, it's up to me to take an action. I have only myself to blame if I don't."

"I would make plans," says Judy, "and then I would follow through on them, no matter what the heck was going down with me. It used to feed my ego, make me feel good about myself, if I could chug along no matter how bad I was feeling. Acting like Superwoman should have made me feel like I could accomplish the impossible, but it did just the opposite because I felt so angry at having to do it all. If I'm not feeling up to par, I moderate my schedule."

"I go to HALT," says Charlene. "I ask myself if I'm hungry, angry, lonely, or tired. It's basic, but that's what I often forget about. There isn't one of those that I can't take care of with some action of my own part. I can feed myself, I have tools to deal with anger, I can call a friend if I'm lonely, and I can take a nap or got to bed early. In the old days, prior to recovery, I didn't think to take care of myself. I was always taking care of others and waiting for others to take care of me. When they didn't, I thought it was because I wasn't worth taking care of. So no wonder I didn't take care of myself."

"How is the world treating you?" says Judy. "That's a question people ask each other, but it's something I need to ask myself. Did I feel good about that? Did I feel appreciated and loved? Did I feel undervalued today? Did I feel ignored? If the answer is no to any of the above, I have to ask myself, did I make anyone feel appreciated today? Did I show love for anyone? Or did I undervalue someone? Did I ignore someone? What goes around comes around. It's so simple. I don't know why it took me sixty years to learn that."

It's also about our physical health.

"As I get older, I do need to take better care of myself physically," says Hector. "I've tried to stay in denial about that, but the Tenth Step helps me even if I don't want help. If an ache or pain has been going on too long, I know I have to see the doctor."

"I make sure about my diet," says Olga.

"My mother and my sister died of breast cancer," say Charlene. "I was always afraid to do self-examination. Now I do it as a matter of course. It's part of my Tenth Step inventory."

Sometimes the Tenth Step can lead us back to other Steps.

"My son and daughter moved back into the house," says Sally. "I guess even the biggest house in the world isn't big enough for in-laws. Especially if their stay is open-ended. They're broke and it's mostly because they can't rein in their spending. Their situation was becoming the focus of my life. Doing the Tenth Step, I realized it wasn't so much the space they were taking up in my house. It was the space they were taking up in my head. Step Ten led me back to Step One. I am powerless over them and their spending, and it was making my life unmanageable."

And to balance any negative behaviors noted, you could also review the positive actions you took today, such as visiting a friend in the hospital, getting some exercise, or doing some community service. Or maybe it was as simple as stopping yourself before you snapped at somebody or offering to sponsor a newcomer at your Twelve Step meeting.

"I try to remember the good things that happened on a given day," says Jowin. "For one thing, my son didn't make any bets today, and that's got to be something to feel good about."

Says Judy, "I used to call it a good day if some major drama ended without the world coming to an end. Nowadays, the dramas in my life are few and far between. I'm grateful for that too. And I'm grateful for things I used to think were too small for me to appreciate. Like seeing my grandchildren having a good time. Or being able to do a small favor for a neighbor."

Along with your inventory of negative feelings, such as resentment, fear, and envy, you might make a mental list of the positive feelings you had today. Did you feel gratitude or happiness for someone else's success? Did something happen that gave you more hope for the future, or did you experience pride in a job well done?

## A Daily Housecleaning

The second part of the Tenth Step is to promptly make amends. That may have seemed like a formidable task—before we did the Eighth and Ninth Steps. But now it's a different story. For one thing, we know how to make amends. For another thing, we know how it helps *us*, not just the person to whom we are making amends.

"Nipping things in the bud is the best thing I ever did," says Hector. "I was inclined to dawdle and postpone. Don't make such a big deal of it, I'd think. It'll go away eventually; everyone forgets. But I never forgot, so I was always waiting for the other shoe to drop. I mean, one thing you learn when you get older is that what goes around comes around. Self-fulfilling prophecies are for real. If I was waiting for the shoe to fall, it almost always did. Now I make amends as soon as I can. I'm not waiting for the other shoe to fall, and it doesn't! It's like a whole new way of life for me."

"Also, the great thing about making prompt amends is that little things don't turn into big things," says Olga. "Most problems start very small. But if you take care of them right away, you really can keep them small."

"Doing the Tenth Step enables me to do damage control," says Jowin, "before there's any damage."

"Inventory," says Robert. "Usually, I do it in the evening. I just go over my day. It takes two or three minutes. It's no big effort. I focus on how I acted with other people. Was I inconsiderate? Did I lose my temper? Was I impatient? Did I overreact to someone or something? That's still a big one for me. My skin hasn't gotten any thicker since I got sober, but the program and time have taught me to watch those reactions. And when I do blow, I make amends right away. And by right away, I mean that day."

"Learning restraint of pen and tongue has been key for me," says Judy. "When I get all wound up, I start making these self-righteous calls to friends or sending them these very critical emails. I told myself I was just being honest, but I was being brutal. It doesn't happen much now that I'm sober, but when it does, I apologize."

"I like the rough-and-tumble of being in the real estate world," says Olga. "I can be overly aggressive. I used to say that's how real estate works. If you can't stand the heat . . . ! But when I do the Tenth Step, I see that I lie sometimes and call it doing business. The Tenth Step helps me see that. Before the end of the day, I'm on the phone, correcting whatever 'misinformation' I've given to a buyer or a seller."

"Even though I made my Ninth Step amends for lying, I still catch myself doing it sometimes," says Jowin. "The Tenth Step helps me stick to the amends I made before. I really feel as though it's helping to remap my brain here and change my behavior."

Step Ten helps us keep the focus on the "now." The Tenth Step can teach us to avoid repeating mistakes we have made in the past. We can avoid making new mistakes. And when we do blow it, we can defuse our little bombshells before they explode and do others and ourselves any serious damage.

This is where we really and truly start to add a whole new depth and dimension to living one day at a time.

## STEP ELEVEN

*"Sought through prayer and meditation to improve our conscious contact with God* as we understood Him, *praying only for knowledge of His will for us and the power to carry that out."*

THE ELEVENTH STEP can be a way to gain an appreciation of where we are at in the moment, to renew and reaffirm a sense of purpose and connection with life that some of us may feel ebbing away as we age.

This is a spiritual program, and although we skirted it cautiously at the beginning of our recovery, we now acknowledge a spiritual dimension in our lives. Does that mean we are all believers in a traditional concept of God? Not necessarily. Contrary to what you may have heard, belief in a Higher Power is not blind. It comes in increments more often than not, and, when it comes as a result of systematically working these Steps, we can actually say that it's based on our empirical experience.

If we are thinking and behaving more sanely than we were before we started the Steps, it may well be because we now understand that a Power greater than ourselves can restore us to sanity. That was the Second Step. If we feel saner after taking Step Two, we were more likely to approach Step Three with more conviction, more openness, more willingness. If we found that turning our life and our will over to the care of a Higher Power loosens our ego's hold on our feelings, we were likelier to be willing to let a Higher Power remove our shortcomings when we got to Step Seven.

We have learned that beliefs come in all sorts of shapes and sizes. One size does not fit all. We all have our differences, and they are reflected in our many different understandings of what a Higher Power is and can be. No longer do we compare our beliefs with anyone else's.

If there's one thing we do share, it's our comprehension—finally and consciously—that we are not our own Higher Power. That's a major development. Even if we never consciously thought of ourselves as God—and who does, except mentally ill people with delusions of grandeur?—our behavior and our feelings in the past have suggested otherwise. At some time in our lives, we designated substances and pleasure-seeking behaviors as our Higher Power and turned our will and our live over to drugs, alcohol, gambling, food, or other addictions.

## Seeking Our Higher Power's Will

"I was a foxhole believer. 'Oh, God, get me out of this mess and I promise I'll never do crystal meth again.' But I always did it again," says Craig. "When I started working the Steps, my sponsor told me praying was talking to my Higher Power; meditating was listening. It was a whole different experience for me. Now I have a whole different relationship with my Higher Power."

Charlene grew up believing in a Higher Power, but one who was vengeful, punishing, cold, and impersonal. "My Higher Power didn't know me from a hole in the wall, except when I was bad and had to be punished," she explains. "The more I do the Eleventh Step, the more clearly I feel the presence of a Higher Power that takes a personal interest in me, loves me, and provides me with what I need."

Once we make conscious contact with our Higher Power, however, it's all too easy not to make a regular habit of it. Because things are better, because we're not using or behaving addictively any more, we may think we don't need our Higher Power any more. But the truth is we can profit from continuous application of Step Eleven.

"I'd been sober a long time," says Olga. "But when I got to my fifties, I began to wonder what the point was in seeking knowledge of what my Higher Power's will for me was. I mean, most of the things that I was supposed to do are already done, are already accomplished. I try to behave well, be considerate, but I didn't think there was anything new for me to learn from doing the Eleventh Step. Getting into the Step study group helped me realize how I would benefit from doing this Step on a regular basis."

Jowin agrees. "Doing the Eleventh Step is how I found out that I have a lot still left to do in life," he explains. "All my life I knew what I was going to do. I was going to go through school and get a job and get married and have children. Now the kids are grown and I'm working less. This is the first time in my life when I don't have a plan. It's through practicing the Eleventh Step that I found out it's not so much what I do but how I do it."

Says Hector. "I've been running around all my life, trying to get all my wants satisfied. Now I'm bored with my agenda. My doctor says it's mild depression. My friends are well-meaning, but their suggestions don't help. I kept asking my Higher Power about the future, and what I kept hearing was that I need to focus on the present. That's really changed the way I look at my life. It also got me out of my depression."

"I got more than my share of the American dream," says Robert. "I like the toys and prizes. I thought I needed every single one of them. But I have to admit I feel disappointed they haven't made me as happy as I was expecting. Truth is that I was confusing getting the things I want with the things I need."

"Knowing that all my needs are met is what my Higher Power wants for me," says Sally. "As I work the Eleventh Step, my Higher Power teaches me the differences between what I want and what I need. It's a process, and I learn it again and again. I'm also learning to be grateful and also how to accept losses when they occur."

## Spiritual Growth

Although we may become more acutely aware of loss as we enter our fifties and sixties, the truth is that we all experience losses of one kind or another throughout our lives. As we grow from one stage of life to another, we leave things behind, sometimes by choice, but sometimes not. Sometimes we outgrow them, of course.

It's how we grow emotionally and, as noted by Erik Erikson, a pioneer in developmental psychology, it's how we grow spiritually. Think, for a moment, of all the things you needed when you were an infant that you didn't need when you became a child. What were the "necessities" of childhood that you put behind you when you were an adolescent? Certain toys? Certain ways of behaving? Certain beliefs? Weren't you relieved when you found you didn't need to be the most popular kid in school, or the cutest, or the brightest? How did it feel when you realized you didn't need so much attention, power, or control? How many of us have realized that the money and position we strived for had, in time, become obstacles on our path to serenity? For those of us with substance use disorders, can you remember how you thought you could not live without drugs and alcohol—only to find you could live much better without them?

## Aging, Loss, and Acceptance

But no matter how liberating some of those losses can be, the prospect of aging can signal the biggest and, for many of us, the most dreaded losses. That's something we can't deny or ignore, especially now.

More and more, we suffer the loss of people who are dear to

us. Our parents, if they are still alive, may be beginning to fail. Some of our friends, too, have passed on, and others have simply moved out of our lives, unlikely to return. Tragically, some of us may have also experienced the loss of a child.

We may find that it's time to leave the home we have lived in for many years. Many of us scale down at this time—for a variety of reasons. As we do that, we are often saying good-bye to neighbors as well as to a community.

Many of us are saying good-bye to jobs. Retirement, or cutting down from full-time employment, is a loss too. And not just financially. All too many of us retirees feel pushed out of work before our time, but even those of us who opt out of the workforce often feel some loss of prestige and purpose.

"After I retired I lost my identity," says Robert. "That's part of the reason I had a slip. Getting sober again was the key, but it's really conscious contact with my Higher Power that reminds me I have a course in life: I am a human being, not just a 'human doing.'"

Financial reverses, employment-related or not, are difficult for anyone at any time, but they may be especially challenging for us Boomers. Over the years, some of us have been able to establish such financial security that we may see many of our wants as total necessities. When the economic picture worldwide becomes more precarious, our fear of loss can overwhelm us.

Even the least vain of us experiences some sense of loss as our bodies age. We may not have the physical strength we had before, or the stamina. Even if we are not vain, we can feel a sense of loss as our appearance changes. Our skin changes, our hair, the shape of our bodies.

"Forty was a downer," says Judy. "Turning sixty was more like the world was coming to an end. I filled my time with being furious at my ex-husband and having cosmetic surgery. It honestly didn't occur to me that there was going to be more to my life than that. It was through working the Eleventh Step that I realized that God had more in store for me than that."

Most treacherous, however, is the loss of our health. Sometimes, of course, our health can be a major crisis, but more often than not, health issues surface through a slow process that we only detect over a period of time.

"I was diagnosed with breast cancer a few months after I started working the Steps," Olga reminds us. "I had surgery. It came back. I had chemo. It came back. I was devastated. My health obviously isn't so great. But I found that I am able to live my life and enjoy it too—one day at a time. It turned out that good health wasn't a necessity. But I wouldn't have been able to do that if I didn't have conscious contact with a Higher Power who loves me and cares for me, even when I'm sick. That's not something I ever wanted to know. But at this stage of the game, it's something I needed to know, and I found it out through working the Eleventh Step."

## A New Understanding of Time

Our ability to plan and defer gratification is one way we deal with time, and that can be a real asset, especially when we're young. Waiting to buy something till we have the money, for instance, can save us a lot of grief. Who doesn't admire people who can postpone something they'd like to do so that they can help someone else? But when deferral becomes a way of life, it's something else again. While we are always in the process of becoming, we also learn how to focus on how we become each day, not over a period of weeks or months or years.

"I was waiting for my father to die," says Sally. "Everything was on hold. It was a terrible way to live. I brought it to my Higher Power when I was doing the Eleventh Step. 'What am I supposed to do?' I kept asking. That was my prayer. The answer I heard was 'Live in the moment.' It didn't seem like the answer I was looking for at the time, but it was the answer I needed. This is how I learned that my Higher Power had better plans for me than anything I could imagine for myself. After I realized that, it was easy for me to do the Eleventh Step."

Says Hector, "You know how you look at the clock and it's almost time to go home or go to sleep, and you tell yourself it's too late to start something? That's how I was with my life. I just thought it was too late to start anything. My Higher Power was the one who said it isn't. There were some things I wanted to do, but I'd decided I couldn't because I wouldn't have time to finish them. I decided it was irresponsible for me to get a dog because he might outlive me, and then what would happen?"

"When a man took an interest in me," says Olga, "I laughed. Dating, maybe getting into a relationship, isn't what I was planning for this stage of life. Why would anyone my age want to do that? Well, people my age do get lonely, do need companionship, still enjoy sex. My Higher Power wants me to be happy, joyous, and free. Step Eleven reminds me I'm still a very human being."

"Time can be a preoccupation for many of us," says Mack. "I know I can become depressed, morbid about it. But when I work the Eleventh Step, I know that's not what my Higher Power wants for me. If you think your Higher Power wants you to be miserable, it's time to get a new Higher Power! How do you do that? By working the Eleventh Step and expanding your conscious contact!"

"Before I did the Eleventh Step, I was becoming preoccupied with death and how little time I had left," says Sally. "When a friend died, my first thought was, 'I'm next.' That was no way to live. When I do the Eleventh Step, I know that time is precious and to make the most of each day. If I'm doing that, I don't worry about how much time there is left for me."

"Life can be hard," says Olga. "Sometimes I use the Eleventh Step as refuge from it. Sometimes I will come out of a meditation session knowing just what I need to do about something. But more often than not, it's just a lovely place to go. It's sort of my alternative universe, and I can go there regardless. Most places I go, I need my car or a friend. Or I need money or whatever. I just can't get there without help. With the Eleventh Step, it's always there, and the more I do it, the more aware I am that it's not a 'there,' it's here—and it always was!"

"I guess I take inventory too much," says Robert. "Does it all add up? Was it enough? Should it be more? Working the Eleventh Step, I hear my Higher Power telling me that I'm exactly where I'm supposed to be, who I'm supposed to be, what I'm supposed to be. That's all I need, isn't it?"

No matter what the state of our identities, our looks, even our health, no matter what are losses are, working Step Eleven can remind us that we are loved and whole and perfect. It gives us a simple, time-proven method for knowing what to do next in good times and bad, by tapping into our Higher Power's will for us, from moment to moment, day to day. Thanks to Step Eleven, we can appreciate that in a spiritual sense, the past and the future are really all contained in this moment, in this day when we live in "the sunlight of the spirit."

# STEP TWELVE

*"Having had a spiritual awakening as the result of these steps, we tried to carry this message to alcoholics, and to practice these principles in all our affairs."*

CARRYING THE MESSAGE IN AA doesn't mean proselytizing. In fact, Bill Wilson often made the point that Alcoholics Anonymous works through attraction rather than promotion. That's how it works for all the other Twelve Step programs too. One can only imagine how many suffering souls out there have been turned off and fled from men and women who tried to "convert" them to the Twelve Steps.

"Someone tried to convert me," says Olga. "One of the women who worked for me was always throwing her sobriety in as many faces as she could. From time to time, I would receive AA brochures in the mail. Anonymous. But I suspected they were from the woman. I can tell you I built up quite a resentment. It just made me more adamant about not going to a meeting."

Even when people have the best of intentions, promotion can backfire. "I tried to Twelve-Step my daughter," says Mack. "It was a big mistake. When I told my sponsor, he explained it almost never works with family. The best you can do is be available. People are ready when they are ready. That's how it was for me."

Not only can you offend the dearest people in your life, but you can also do yourself some damage if you don't think first. "I heard about a guy who went to Twelve-Step someone who was in detox," says Craig. "He even got the person to give him the pills he had on him. But on the way out of the detox unit, instead of throwing the pills in the garbage, the guy took them. Imagine, he had a slip on a Twelfth Step call. One lesson is you shouldn't do it on your own. Take someone from your fellowship."

The Twelve Steps are a very practical basis for living. The point is that they work. Be mindful, though, that they don't work for everyone. If it works for you but not your best friends, it's not necessarily because you are brighter or work harder or that God loves you more.

"I hear people saying, oh, so-and-so isn't ready for a program," says Hector. "That's kind of patronizing, I think. The programs aren't for everyone. As they say at meetings, the Twelve Steps aren't for people who need them. They're for people who want them."

## Be Grateful, Be Humble

Gratitude and humility can be a challenge for anyone at any age, but the older we get, the more entitled some of us may feel about the "superior" wisdom that is born of old age. We may feel impelled to share it, especially with younger people, whether or not others want to hear. We may feel resentful and even indignant when our deep insights and sage advice are ignored or rejected.

The first part of Step Twelve can save us a lot of grief in this area: "Having had a spiritual awakening as a result of these steps . . ." It's rare for a spiritual awakening to take the form of a dramatic white-light experience, such as Bill Wilson's when he finally hit bottom with his drinking. For most of us, the awakening is the experience of deep humility that comes from working the first eleven Steps and the new sense of gratitude we gain from our new ability to be of service to others—which is where Step Twelve comes in. We find out what people mean when they say that this is a selfish program, that we reach out to other people who still suffer as much to keep ourselves clean and sober as to help them. Their help ultimately comes from *their* Higher Power, just as ours did.

"It took me a while to understand that the message isn't that the other person can or should get sober too," says Robert. "It isn't even for me to tell other people they ought to have a spiritual awakening. People get into trouble when they substitute other messages."

"I know I offended some very dear friends," says Sally. "I lost almost a hundred pounds in OA and I've managed to keep them off. What's even more important is that after I stabilized, I kept getting saner and saner in my eating habits as well as the rest of my life. I think I meant well when I'd tell my friends who were overweight that they should go to OA, but I was also sending a message: that they'd be better if they were more like me."

So the message, clearly, isn't about what *you* think other people need or what *you* can do for them. The message is that you, and thousands like you, have found a program that has given you a new freedom—and it's there for anyone who wants what you have and is willing to give the Steps a try.

## Don't Tell—Show

The truth is, you don't so much tell others what the program's about and what it can do for them. You show them. It's a program that works by attraction rather than promotion. We work it by example.

"That's how it worked for me," says Olga. "A distant relative, the wife of a second cousin, as a matter of fact. I'd see her once or twice a year at family weddings. I noticed how much better she looked, how much happier she seemed. I asked her what was going on, and she said she'd joined AA. That was it. A week later I went to my first meeting."

"Someone was making amends to me," explains Charlene. "I didn't see the point, frankly, and was fairly dismissive. But I could see over the next few months how our relationship was changing. I wanted to gossip and complain the way we always had, and she just wasn't interested. I could see she was outgrowing me. That made me think."

That's the way it has worked in all the other Twelve Steps programs as well. No wonder. People who "promote" spiritual paths or self-improvement programs can be irritating or scary and sometimes both. How often have we witnessed men and women claiming some kind of spirituality or higher principle to justify some very unspiritual, unprincipled, violent, and cruel actions? Although it's easy to distinguish ourselves from them, we may need to check our own motives when we are carrying the message—and what message we are actually carrying.

"I had several sponsees who were in their early twenties," says Robert. "I was always trying to get them to go back to college or get a decent job with good medical benefits. They came from blue-collar families, and I thought it was my job to get them into white-collar careers."

"I thought everyone would be happier if they believed in the same Higher Power I believed in," says Charlene. "I know I'm happier, but I have some humility now and I know it wouldn't necessarily make anyone else happier."

"I had a sponsor who told me I could pass for straight," says Craig. "He meant it as a compliment too. I explained to him that I never wanted to be straight. He had a hard time believing that, but it's true. Even so, I used to wonder sometimes if black people don't wish they were white, or Catholics don't wish they were Protestant. Since I am white and Protestant, I realized I'd been doing in my mind what that man was doing out loud."

"I used to sponsor a gal in her twenties," says Sally. "A nice person with a very good program too. I didn't have to convert her to that. But I was always giving her advice on how she should raise her kids and how she should deal with her husband. I was trying to help her circumvent the problems I'd had when I was her age. She never took any of my advice, and I resented it. When I told her how I felt, she complained that I was trying to put a sixty-year-old head on her twenty-eight-year-old shoulders. I think she was right too."

## Many Paths, One Goal

And so it goes. All too often we think people will be better off if only they dressed as we do, spoke as we do, believed and acted as we do. Some people seem to think the world would be at peace if we were all the same color, the same religion, and the same ethnic background. Sometimes our differences can blind us to our central task of working toward our mutual benefit in meeting a higher purpose or goal. It happens with families all the time. It even happens in the Twelve Step world.

If you've ever attended the business meeting of a Twelve Step program, you can picture how two people who were in utter harmony about sobriety during the meeting can't agree on what kind of cake to serve at the group's anniversary: they have to flip a coin to decide. Most of us who were around in the 1980s remember that smoking at meetings became an extraordinarily divisive issue—until smoking was banned in most of the public places where AA groups met.

"Learning to tolerate other people's differences without feeling that one is jeopardizing one's own principles is another major step in the right direction," says Jowin. "That is one of the main things I have learned through the Steps. I can afford to let people have their own opinions, feelings, whatever. I have my share of imperfections, but I understand in a spiritual sense that, imperfect as I may be, I am whole, complete. That's my spiritual awakening, and I try to treat people, imperfect as they are, as whole, complete people."

Says Mack, "I don't know why bad things happen to good people. I don't even really know why bad things happen to bad people, but I do believe in a benevolent, loving Higher Power who loves me no matter what I do and will help me get through whatever it is that I am going through. The way I carry that message is to treat people in a loving manner, no matter what they are going through or dealing with."

"It's about being enough as is," says Olga. "Of course, it's a message that anyone can carry at any time, but I think that people our age have a certain authority here. We've been through times when we thought we weren't enough, when we didn't actually have enough, but we got through them."

"I don't need to be in control," says Robert. "That's the biggest gift the Twelve Steps have brought me. I was in control at work because I was the boss. I was in control at home because I was the breadwinner. Now I'm not the boss. I'm not the breadwinner. I don't have a whole lot of strings to pull any more. It was a total surprise that the world would go on if I weren't in control. I'm amazed. That's a message I can carry to people."

"I didn't reach all my goals careerwise," says Jowin. "I thought I'd just keep plugging away at them till I got there. But as I worked the Steps, I realized that dreams change. I'm still working, but I have different goals now and they have nothing to do with how much money I make or what position I have at work."

"I bought into my mother's picture of happiness," says Charlene. "When my husband died, I thought I'd have to remarry if I was going to be happy. But when I did the Steps, I realized I was always saying I'd be happy when I get this or when I do that. But I want to be happy as I am now, which happens to be single. Thanks to the Steps, I found the tools I need to do that. Who I am. That's my spiritual awakening."

"Of course, I want to be of service," says Sally. "People think that old people have so much time on their hands. That's not necessarily true. Like a lot of us, I still have to work. I resented that at first. It's not a choice. It's a necessity. But now, thanks to the Steps, I see it as how my path was meant to go, and I am supposed to make the best of it. I can see already that if it weren't for my work, I might have disappeared into my apartment watching TV."

"I love my grandchildren and I like spending time with them, but I don't want to spend this part of life sitting for them because my daughter doesn't want to spend the money for daycare," says Charlene. "I felt guilty, but the Steps helped me realize that being of service doesn't mean I have to be anyone's servant."

"What I want to be is excellent," says Judy. "I always did the minimum I could get by with. I think it was my way of making sure no one judged me too severely. I was always saying, 'If only I'd had more time, I could have cooked a better meal, or taken really good care of my home, or spent more time with friends, or been more considerate.' It was a cop-out, I see. Now I do my best. A lot of the time I'm fine with it. But when I'm not, I don't make excuses. It's about making the most of what I have. It's about saying I'm enough, it's enough, you're enough. As someone who spent most of her life saying nothing was enough, this is an incredible change. It's liberation for me. It's the gift I receive daily from practicing the Steps to the best of my ability, and that's the message I want to carry."

"I was a perfectionist," says Hector. "I just wasn't happy with anything. Now I let it go. I can move on now."

We all have different paths. For some, it's to become excellent. For others, it's to chill in the perfectionism department. Some of us need to let go of control. Others feel it's time to affirm their authority. It's all about continuing the process, being alive. As one Twelve-Stepper said, "I want to die young at a very old age."

Says Robert, "As I practice these principles in all my affairs, I'm finding that the reward is in the act of doing the right thing. I feel more comfortable with myself and with other people. I feel that every problem has a solution. It's about living one day at a time, no matter what age you are. It's taken me a heap of living as well as all Twelve Steps to really get it. And I'm still learning, still growing. Some people say no one ever really changes, but I have, and so have a lot of other men and women who follow the Twelve Steps. Over the years, I have seen thousands of them too."

Turning sixty or seventy, or any age, doesn't have to be the beginning of the end. In many ways, we've been fortunate to have the kinds of life problems and maladies that brought us to a Twelve Step program, no matter when that happens or how many times we return after having left. And with the humility and gratitude that we've gained through the daily renewal of our programs, we can continue to be of service—to newcomers at meetings, to our loved ones, to everyone we meet. With the Twelve Steps as a guide and a lifetime of experience under our belts, every day can bring a new lease on life.

# The Twelve Steps of Alcoholics Anonymous*

1. We admitted we were powerless over alcohol—that our lives had become unmanageable.
2. Came to believe that a Power greater than ourselves could restore us to sanity.
3. Made a decision to turn our will and our lives over to the care of God *as we understood Him.*
4. Made a searching and fearless moral inventory of ourselves.
5. Admitted to God, to ourselves, and to another human being the exact nature of our wrongs.
6. Were entirely ready to have God remove all these defects of character.
7. Humbly asked Him to remove our shortcomings.
8. Made a list of all persons we had harmed, and became willing to make amends to them all.
9. Made direct amends to such people wherever possible, except when to do so would injure them or others.
10. Continued to take personal inventory and when we were wrong promptly admitted it.
11. Sought through prayer and meditation to improve our conscious contact with God *as we understood Him,* praying only for knowledge of His will for us and the power to carry that out.
12. Having had a spiritual awakening as the result of these steps, we tried to carry this message to alcoholics, and to practice these principles in all our affairs.

*The Twelve Steps of AA are taken from *Alcoholics Anonymous,* 4th ed., published by AA World Services, Inc., New York, NY, 59–60.

# The Serenity Prayer

God, grant me the serenity
To accept the things I cannot change,
The courage to change the things I can,
And the wisdom to know the difference.

# The Seventh Step Prayer*

My Creator, I am now willing that you should have all of me, good and bad. I pray that you now remove from me every single defect of character which stands in the way of my usefulness to you and my fellows. Grant me strength, as I go out from here, to do your bidding. Amen.

*The Seventh Step Prayer is taken from *Alcoholics Anonymous*, 4th ed., published by AA World Services, Inc., New York, NY, 76.

# About the Author

**Stephen Roos** was born in New York, grew up in Connecticut, and graduated from Yale. He worked in publishing for ten years before turning to writing. Since then he has published two dozen books, including many novels for adults and young adults. He is author of *A Young Person's Guide to the Twelve Steps*, published by Hazelden.

He currently lives in northwest Connecticut.

**Hazelden,** a national nonprofit organization founded in 1949, helps people reclaim their lives from the disease of addiction. Built on decades of knowledge and experience, Hazelden offers a comprehensive approach to addiction that addresses the full range of patient, family, and professional needs, including treatment and continuing care for youth and adults, research, higher learning, public education and advocacy, and publishing.

A life of recovery is lived "one day at a time." Hazelden publications, both educational and inspirational, support and strengthen lifelong recovery. In 1954, Hazelden published *Twenty-Four Hours a Day,* the first daily meditation book for recovering alcoholics, and Hazelden continues to publish works to inspire and guide individuals in treatment and recovery, and their loved ones. Professionals who work to prevent and treat addiction also turn to Hazelden for evidence-based curricula, informational materials, and videos for use in schools, treatment programs, and correctional programs.

Through published works, Hazelden extends the reach of hope, encouragement, help, and support to individuals, families, and communities affected by addiction and related issues.

For questions about Hazelden publications,
please call **800-328-9000**
or visit us online at **hazelden.org/bookstore**.